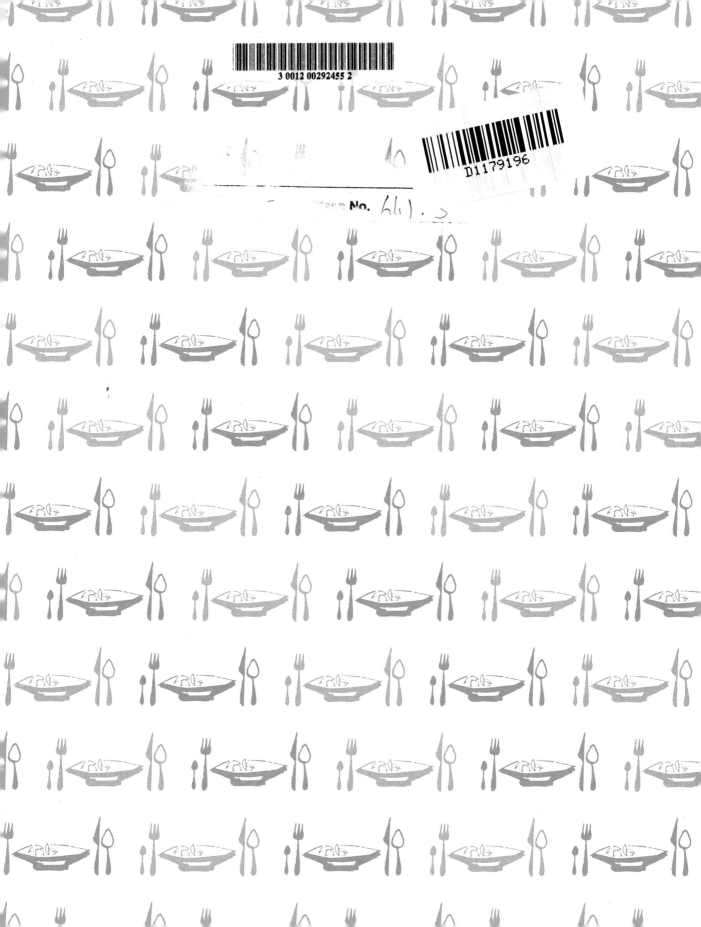

No. 641.

About the Author

Simon Dougan was born in south Armagh. He has worked as a chef all his adult life, first in London and then back home in Northern Ireland. Having run the kitchen of an enormously successful restaurant for six years, he decided he wanted to make and sell the kind of food that he loved eating every day, so he opened The Yellow Door Deli in Portadown in 1998. Since then the company has gone from strength to strength – another deli opened in Belfast in 2000 and the company has also become Northern Ireland's number one outside catering business, providing food of the highest quality for hundreds of high-profile events every year. This is Simon's first book.

The Yellow Door

our story
our recipes

641.5

blackstaff press belfast

First published in 2008 by Blackstaff Press
4c Heron Wharf
Sydenham Business Park
Belfast BT3 9LE

A CIP catalogue record for this book is
available from the British Library.

Food photography: Clíona O'Flaherty
Design: Keith Connolly at Tonic
Food stylist: Sharon Hearne-Smith
Photographer's assistant: Aoife Herrity
Food stylist's assistant: Barbara Nealon

Printed in Italy by Sedit

ISBN 978-0-85640-828-1

www.blackstaffpress.com
www.yellowdoordeli.co.uk

With thanks to Marks and Spencers,
Debenhams and Murphy Sheehy Fabrics
for the loan of props for photography.

Con-tents

Conversion Charts vi

Using This Book vii

The Yellow Door: A Not-So-Brief History . . ix

Breakfasts 1

Deli Favourites 21

First Courses 51

Main Courses 85

The End of the Meal 123

Parties 157

Directory 183

Index 186

People Who Inspire Me 190

Conversion Charts

Oven temperatures

DEGREES CENTIGRADE

140°	150°	170°	180°	190°	200°	220°	230°	240°
1	2	3	4	5	6	7	8	9

GAS MARK

Measurements

CENTIMETRES

0.3	0.5	1	2	2.5	3	4	4.5	5	7.5
⅛	¼	½	¾	1	1¼	1½	1¾	2	3

INCHES

CENTIMETRES

10	13	15	18	20	23	25	28	30	35
4	5	6	7	8	9	10	11	12	14

INCHES

Using this Book

Always use free-range eggs. Go for free-range meat, too; and organic, if you can find it.

Choose organic salmon.

Buy local, seasonal ingredients, and remember to support your local suppliers.

All herbs are fresh, unless the recipe says otherwise. And while we are on the subject of fresh herbs, I would urge you to grow your own. You can grow them on your windowsill, in an old biscuit tin with holes in the bottom or even in a grow bag. You'll save money and, more importantly, have plenty to cook with. It's almost impossible to add too many herbs when you're cooking, so you'll have no trouble using them up.

Always use unrefined sugar.

All recipes need whole milk, unless otherwise stated.

Please bear in mind that oven temperatures vary from model to model. It's important to follow the manufacturer's instructions, and to get to know your own oven.

The Yellow Door
A Not-So-Brief History

Back in 1992 I came home from London for a short break, having worked there for four years. I was looking forward to a few weeks off, far from the hustle and bustle of city life – some time to gather my thoughts, before continuing my career as a hungry young chef.

While at home I was asked to help out at a small country restaurant in Gilford, which was still trying to find its feet. A little part-time work, I thought; something to keep my hand in and the chance to earn a few quid before using my return ticket back to the big smoke.

The restaurant – Sarah Moon's as it was then called – had been going for many years. It was once an old pub, and had kept something of that atmosphere. It had a reputation for comfortable relaxed dining and was a place where people felt very much at home. This familiar ambience and tranquil feel was a huge part of the restaurant's charm. The building itself was nothing to write home about, with its fake Tudor look and its position on the edge of a busy road. However, once inside, guests relaxed on mismatched settees and soft seats in gentle lighting.

The new owner, Roisin Hendron, had just returned from London, too, and had experienced the same modern styles as me. We shared a passion for good, honest, high quality food. Roisin didn't have experience of being a chef, or of running a busy restaurant kitchen, and that's where I came in. This was my new short-term position.

In 1992, food in Northern Ireland was very different. It seems laughable now but orange juice was a staple first course at most hotels; prawn cocktail was one of the smartest dishes on any menu; and boiled eggs, accompanied by all kinds of colourful versions of mayonnaise and served with soggy round lettuce, tomato wedges and mustard cress, were everywhere.

> I was starting to enjoy the feeling of creating new dishes, ones that didn't involve tomato wedges and the afore-mentioned mustard cress on the side of each plate.

So at Sarah Moon's the first thing to change was the menu. We didn't do anything too daring at first, really just making the regular dishes a little bit smarter. Maybe it was the look of the plates as they arrived on tables, maybe it was the depth of flavour in the sauces and accompaniments, maybe it was just the freshness of the ingredients on our small menu, or maybe it was the fact that each dish was being cooked to order. Whatever the reason, we were quickly up and running. The popularity of the restaurant and its reputation for good food grew very quickly.

I was starting to enjoy the feeling of creating new dishes, ones that didn't involve tomato wedges and the afore-mentioned mustard cress on the side of each plate. I delayed my return to London, and the helping-out position for a few hours a week, which I flippantly took on, turned into a helping-out position of more than sixty hours a week. Much to the delight of my family, and especially my mum, I decided to stay on, at least for a while, to see how things would pan out (if you can excuse the pun). After just a few short weeks, the restaurant was much noisier and busier at night, with even more eager diners, and the phone rang a lot more than it used to.

I soon needed help in the kitchen. Through a friend of a friend, Roisin got in touch with Noel Doran, a catering lecturer who plied his trade in a classroom in Omagh College, and he came to the rescue. Enter Michael Donaghy, a fresh-faced and eager student of Noel's who was showing great promise. He hailed from Clogher in County Tyrone – a country boy just like me. We were now a team, sort of. Noel helped again by gathering together a collection of other, slightly spottier, individuals to peel vegetables and throw water over plates and themselves. A very young rag-tag bunch, but we thought we were invincible. Roisin worked out front, taking orders with her new Portuguese sidekick, Hernani Oliveira – Nani. His

The one thing we always remembered was only to use the freshest and best ingredients. This is still at the core of our business and just as important now as it ever was.

English was a bit ropey and he stood out, being the only non-pale face for miles around. With his sun-kissed looks and friendly and helpful disposition, he was our man in Havana. The team was really beginning to gel. We had conscripts from Derry and even a few Dutch members, in the form of some nice young ladies whom Roisin's contacts in London had directed to us. At least they kept us hormone-charged youths perky.

We now thought it was time to rename the restaurant, putting our own stamp on it. Deliberation started on Tuesday and by Friday, like the politicians of the day, we were no further on – no one could agree on anything. It was starting to become tedious. At last, Roisin – who had painted the front door the previous week – said, 'Let's just call it The Yellow Door.' No one could think of anything better. The name stuck.

The whole place now had a real buzz. The food was getting more exciting and we were learning and becoming more confident, taking our inspiration from many sources, such as the mountains of cookery books we had at our disposal. Marco Pierre White was a god, Raymond Blanc a trusted ally. At first we copied some of the recipes, then we adapted them and finally we created our own. The one thing we always remembered was only to use the freshest and best ingredients. This is still at the core of the business, and just as important now as it ever was.

The Yellow Door restaurant had now matured and found its own way, along with Paul Rankin's fabulous and now Michelin-starred Roscoff's, Michael Deane's excellent eatery in Howard Street and the late great Robbie Millar's restaurant, Shanks. Northern Ireland was beginning to change, not only in culinary terms. People were starting to question the old ways and ask why things had to be the way they were.

We needed premises to pedal our new and simple everyday food to The Yellow Door faithful.

Lunch was always a happy time for us at The Yellow Door. These lunches were some of my most memorable meals; freshly baked bread, simple quiches, boiled Irish ham and mustard, with maybe some salad from the flat roof – not really a roof garden per se, but more a collection of plastic cases, mushrooms boxes and halved olive oil cans in which we grew whatever we could.

We got to thinking that it would be good if we could sell this type of food too. Clearly the restaurant, with its polished service and Villeroy & Boch plates wasn't the forum, so what about a deli? I had read the recipes in the Dean & Deluca cookbook with great gusto. With a rumble in my tummy, I decided that we all had to go to America. Funds were a problem. To do the research in the States, we needed cash. So having discovered the old pub licence was surplus to our requirements, we applied for a restaurant licence and found a buyer for the pub licence. The Robb family was quite eager to sell wine wholesale, so a deal was struck with Philip and Charles. They got the licence and we got round trips to America.

The team took it in turns to go to different establishments in Boston, Chicago and New York. I went to all three cities to see what was hip and happening in the deli world. Michael went to Charlie Trotter's in Chicago, Gordon went to Daniel's in New York, and Nani got stuck in Amsterdam. With no Visa for America anyway, I thought he would be ok. Now with our heads spinning with ideas, we couldn't wait to get started. We needed premises to pedal our new and simple everyday food to The Yellow Door faithful.

At last a little shop in Bridge Street, Portadown, formerly a butcher's shop, became available. The location wasn't great – neither was the shop for that matter – but it did have character, with an original tiled floor and a wooden butcher's block. We loved it, and The Yellow Door Deli was

Food orders for the deli were flying in, the restaurant was booked out for weeks and we were eating Pro Plus and drinking double espressos by the case.

born. The whole idea was to provide customers with the kind of food we enjoyed everyday; not stuffy, not overly lavish, just gutsy, flavoursome, honest food – proper pâtés, delicate desserts with buttery pastry and, of course, really good bread. My job was to cook in the deli in the day and control service at night in the restaurant. Michael was now acting as head chef, a job he was quite capable of doing and doing well. We again enlisted the professional skills of foreigners to help us. Raye the baker was a 4ft barrel of a man with an afro hairstyle. He was of French/Filipino origin and an absolute genius with bread. Like all geniuses he was a little close to the edge. He would fit right into our team.

The Yellow Door Deli was a real culinary emporium. The shop was bursting with all kinds of delicacies. We cooked all day without much concept of stock, or the quantities of food needed to fill our three little counters. Some of it may have gone to waste, but it all looked great and, more importantly, tasted terrific. Everything was really rocking and rolling when Raye went a little too crazy and had to leave. Now that I was the baker, the chef and the dishwasher, things became even crazier – both the deli and the restaurant were at their peak. Food orders for the deli were flying in, the restaurant was booked out for weeks and we were eating Pro Plus and drinking double espressos by the case. This was becoming too much, so I decided to stay on at the deli and sell the restaurant. Roisin had plans to sell her handmade desserts to the restaurant trade, so selling the restaurant would release her to do this, as well as providing the money to set up her operation, which she would run independently. Barry Smith, a young, extremely talented Keady man, arrived on the scene. He had worked with me in the past and was eager to take the already-busy restaurant to the next level. He was aiming for the stars, the Michelin stars.

That nervous feeling I get before an event is still as strong today as it has always been. I suppose it means that I still care. When it gets easy, I'll give up.

I settled into the deli, pouring my heart and soul into it. It was all mine now and it had to work. Some of the team remained in Gilford with Barry but we all stayed very close.

Our first wedding party came not long after. A new concept for me – bring your food, your staff, your kitchen and, yes, even the kitchen sink to a tent in a field. What a logistical nightmare, but it was the adrenaline rush that I enjoyed.

The challenge of recreating restaurant food for a hundred or more guests and serving it to them hot, fresh, and looking and tasting great. The buzz was brilliant, even if the experience was slightly nerve-wracking, to say the least. That nervous feeling I get before an event is still as strong today as it has always been. I suppose it means that I still care. When it gets easy, I'll give up.

I started selling food at Belfast's Farmers Market. The stall was so popular that we decided to set up a satellite deli on the Lisburn Road. Andrew, my cousin and new partner, was a former London Irish player with a passion for good food. He was a big lad with big ideas.

Our little deli in Bridge Street was becoming more and more cramped. We needed bigger and better premises and moved to our current home in Woodhouse Street, Portadown. But before that I had something very special to do – get married. Jilly from Moyallon Foods, who always had a twinkle in her eye when she delivered her excellent beef, pork and wild boar, was to be my soul mate. We had so much in common: a love of food, farming, flavour and fun.

The new premises in Woodhouse Street seemed cavernous, with more than seventy seats in the restaurant downstairs, and two large kitchens and lots of storage and

I have found a new passion – growing my own produce, because freshness has always been the key to producing good food.

office space upstairs. It was to be our new home and from the day it opened it was a success. I loved the hustle and bustle of this much bigger eatery. There was a very positive buzz about the place, with familiar faces visiting even more often now, regulars such as Joe the Bookie, the Tuesday Club, the Trouser Gang from next door and many other friends and loyal supporters.

The little shop in Belfast was also flying and people wanted to take us home – home to do parties, family celebrations, christenings, weddings and business events. The demand for our quickly growing outside catering service was staggering, and I have to say it always feels very special to be part of someone's wedding, or a family's special celebration. I enjoy the planning, the brainstorming and, most of all the food chat. I have met and cooked for some really lovely people over the years, some of whom have become good friends. I have catered weddings for two and sometimes three sisters from the same family – you start to build up a bond with these people like a trusted friend, and it feels good. All these parties and celebrations remind me of the reason why I feel so passionately about my job, and why I began cooking in the first place. I love people, I love fun and I love food.

Today, as The Yellow Door continues to flourish, I have found a new passion – growing my own produce, because freshness has always been the key to producing good food. And as I start on this new adventure, which allows me to take the food from field to platter, I know it will make our food even better, tastier and fresher. Being a chef is not just a job to me, it is an all-consuming way of life.

I hope this book can inspire others in the way that I have been inspired by the love of really good food.

Break-fasts

Baked Breakfast Mushrooms or 'While-Getting-the-Papers' Breakfast / Smoked Salmon and Scrambled Eggs / The Full Irish Breakfast / Baker's Breakfast / Bacon and Cooleeney 'Sort of' Croissants / Almond Croissants / Potato and Causeway Cheese Pancakes / Fried Banana and Maple Syrup on Toast / French Toast, Bacon and Maple Syrup / Strawberry Jam / Rose Petal Jam / Raspberry and White Chocolate Muffins / Bloody Mary / Late Night Breakfast: The Bean, Bacon, Egg and Whatever-is-in-the-Fridge Baked Fry

Baked Breakfast Mushrooms or 'While-Getting-the-Papers' Breakfast

This quick and tasty breakfast cooks while you get the Sunday papers and is the perfect way to impress your partner with your culinary prowess. These mushrooms are also delicious with some crisp pancetta or bacon on the side.

4 large flat-cap mushrooms

2 tbsp olive oil, plus extra for drizzling

salt and freshly ground black pepper

leaves from 1 rosemary sprig, roughly chopped

25g butter

100g Wicklow Blue, St Killian or soft brie-like cheese, sliced into 1cm wedges

4 slices focaccia bread

SERVES 2

Preheat the oven to 170°C.

Trim the stalks of the mushrooms down almost to the cap. Brush all over with olive oil and season with salt and pepper, then place them face up in an ovenproof dish. Sprinkle the rosemary over the mushrooms and top each with a knob of butter. Place in the oven for 15–20 minutes.

Go out for the papers. Don't talk too long to the shopkeeper or anyone else you meet.

On your return, turn on the coffee machine and preheat the grill to its highest setting. Remove the mushrooms from the oven, and place the cheese on top of them. Place under the grill until the cheese is golden and bubbling. Meanwhile, toast the focaccia in a toaster, or under the grill with the mushrooms.

Arrange the focaccia on two plates. Place the mushrooms on the focaccia, add a quick drizzle of olive oil to each one and away with your breakfast tray. A good start to Sunday morning.

Smoked Salmon and Scrambled Eggs

I know that you will look at this recipe and say, 'God, not that old clanger.' The reason for the demise of this wonderful breakfast dish is the use of really poor quality smoked salmon; also, many people have forgotten how to cook scrambled eggs properly. It is not difficult but just needs patience, gentle cooking and constant stirring. I hereby plead with you to give this dish another chance.

200g best quality smoked salmon

10 eggs, lightly beaten

100ml milk

good knob of butter

salt and freshly ground black pepper

toasted brown or wheaten bread to serve

SERVES 4

Take the salmon out of the fridge and divide it among four plates. Allow it to come up to room temperature while you cook the eggs.

Place the eggs, milk, butter and seasoning in a thick-bottomed pan. Heat the mixture gently, stirring all the time with a wooden spoon – do not move from the stove! Constant stirring will ensure that the eggs have a fine texture. When the eggs are very, very lightly set – the consistency of rice pudding – remove the pan from the heat. The eggs will continue to set from their residual heat, even when they are on your plate.

Spoon the eggs onto the plates with the smoked salmon, add another grind of black pepper and serve immediately with toasted brown or wheaten bread.

The Full Irish Breakfast

What's it all about? What should be in, what should be out and how do you cook the damn thing without burning some part of it? Cooking a full Irish breakfast is complex: there are so many elements, each needs a different cooking time or method and everyone likes eggs cooked a different way. I find cooking breakfast for any more than ten people quite challenging, especially as I'm definitely not a morning person.

The one thing that should never be in question is the quality of the ingredients. For this, and every recipe, always use proper, dry-cure bacon, preferably from rare-breed pigs such as Tamworths, Gloucester Old Spots, Saddlebacks and the like. Avoid the cheap, commercially produced, water-laden, tasteless version that steams in the pan and oozes white gunge. Proper bacon will colour as it cooks, retaining shape and flavour. The sausages should be made from the same pigs, encased in natural skins with a high meat content. And, of course, your eggs must be free-range, preferably organic and definitely very fresh. These core items, accompanied by potato bread and soda farls from your local bakery, will guarantee the ultimate Full Irish.

Cooking the Irish Breakfast

This is my method for cooking a great Irish breakfast. I'm not being prescriptive about the quantities, as this method works just as well when cooking for ten people or two. A big job – not for every day – but definitely worth it once in a while.

flat-cap mushrooms

vine-ripened tomatoes, halved

olive oil or melted butter for cooking

salt and freshly ground black pepper

pork sausages

dry-cure bacon

black pudding, sliced

potato bread

soda farls

eggs

Vital accompaniments

toasted white bread, with lots of Irish butter

mugs of tea

brown sauce or ketchup

Get all the ingredients out so that you don't forget anything. Preheat the oven to 180°C (a good starting temperature). Okay, ready to go.

Place the mushrooms and tomatoes on a large baking tray and drizzle with a little olive oil or melted butter. Season generously and put in the oven. Place another baking tray in the oven at the same time.

Pour a little olive oil into a frying pan. Add the sausages and fry them, turning occasionally, until they are nicely browned. Add the sausages to the mushrooms and tomatoes and return the tray to the oven. Fry the bacon and black pudding in the same frying pan, turning occasionally until lightly browned on both sides, then transfer to the baking tray with the sausages etc. and place in the oven. Reduce the oven temperature to 150°C.

Fry the potato bread and soda farls, again in the same frying pan, adding a little more oil or butter if necessary, until golden brown. Place the breads on the other the hot baking tray that has been warming up in the oven. Put the plates in the oven, turn the oven off, put the kettle on to boil and call for your helpers to make the tea, make the toast and lay the table. Fry the eggs in a clean frying pan and plate up as quickly as possible. Serve immediately.

Baker's Breakfast

It was a crazy French-speaking Filipino who first taught me how to bake bread from France, Italy and even further afield. I borrowed Raye from Harrods some ten years ago to kick off the bread production in my first deli. He, like many artistic people, lived a little close to the edge, if you get my drift. Nonetheless, he was probably one of the most talented individuals I have ever worked with and it is Raye I must thank for getting me started in the art of making real bread.

Raye used the little off-cuts of dough from baking to form the base of this rather rich, quiche-type breakfast. You can use the dough from the simple crusty bread recipe on pages 25–6, or use puff pastry instead (prick it all over with a fork before you put the filling on top).

This is what Raye enjoyed for breakfast after a hard night's work in the bakery. As you can see from the ingredients, there are lots of alternatives and Raye chose from whatever was in the fridge that morning. This fantastically tasty breakfast is definitely not for the faint-hearted – as bakers finishing our 'day's work' (the night shift), we found it was best washed down with a glass of cold beer.

¼ quantity bread dough (pages 25–6)

150ml double cream

200g cheese, grated or thinly sliced (Cheddar, brie, goat's or blue cheese all work well)

1 onion, sliced

2 peppers, deseeded and sliced

150g cooked ham or chicken or peeled cooked prawns, chopped

2–3 tbsp chopped mixed herbs, such as basil, parsley, dill and rosemary

SERVES 4–6

Preheat the oven to 200°C.

Flour the work surface thoroughly, and dust a 30cm square baking tray or roasting tin with flour. Roll out the dough as thinly as possible into a roughly square shape. Place on the baking tray. Using the tips of your fingers fold over the edges a little to make a lip all the way around the dough. Pour the cream over the dough and spread it to the edges. Sprinkle with the cheese and then arrange the other ingredients on top, as if preparing a pizza.

Bake for 20–25 minutes, until the dough is cooked through and the cream has evaporated to a sticky consistency. Cut into pieces to serve.

Bacon and Cooleeney 'Sort of' Croissants

This is an unctuous breakfast but also a slight cheat. Great on a Saturday night at 3 a.m. – if you had the foresight to prepare them before you went out and invited everyone back to yours. If you are that sort of person, make an extra batch and put them in the freezer. God knows, you'll thank me some day.

2 sheets ready-rolled puff pastry, about 425g total weight

brown sauce or ketchup

4 dry-cure bacon rashers

100g Cooleeney cheese or brie, cut into 2cm thick slices

1 egg yolk, lightly beaten

SERVES 4

Preheat the oven to 190°C.

Trim each puff pastry sheet into a 13cm square and then cut these diagonally in half to form two triangles from each sheet. Turn one triangle so that the long side is facing you. Squirt a blob of brown sauce or ketchup into the middle of the pastry triangle. Lay a rasher of bacon on top horizontally, followed by a slice or two of cheese.

Roll the pastry away from you into a fairly tight roll, enclosing the bacon and cheese, and turn the ends in a little to make a crescent shape. Place on a baking sheet and repeat with the other triangles.

Brush the croissants with egg yolk and bake them for 15 minutes, until the pastry is risen and golden, and the croissants are crisp underneath. Alternatively, freeze the uncooked croissants, so that you can produce them from the freezer when you really need them! They take about 20 minutes to cook from frozen.

Almond Croissants

This is a very easy way to transform day-old croissants into something different and scrumptious. The frangipane will keep for a week or so in the fridge, or can be frozen.

4 croissants

50g flaked almonds

200g frangipane

Frangipane

250g butter

250g caster sugar

250g ground almonds

20g plain flour

3 large eggs, beaten

SERVES 4

To make the frangipane, beat the butter and sugar until soft and creamy. Add the ground almonds and flour and mix well. Add the beaten eggs, a third at a time, mixing so that each addition is incorporated completely before adding the next. When the eggs are completely incorporated, chill the mixture until you are ready to use it.

To make the almond croissants, preheat the oven to 200°C.

Divide the 200g of frangipane into four. Roll each piece into a sausage shape and place one piece on top of each croissant. Place the croissants on a baking sheet and bake in the oven for 5 minutes. Sprinkle with the flaked almonds and return to the oven for a further 15 minutes, or until the frangipane has run down the sides of the croissants, resembling a comfy duvet. Serve immediately.

Potato and Causeway Cheese Pancakes

These pancakes are perfect for brunch or a light lunch, served with grilled black pudding, crisp streaky bacon, poached eggs and peppery rocket leaves. Top with wholegrain mustard crème fraîche, made by mixing 1 tsp wholegrain mustard into 3 tsp crème fraîche. Alternatively, serve them as a vegetarian option, with field mushrooms, simply grilled with a knob of butter and some fresh thyme. Delish.

500g King Edward potatoes or other floury variety, peeled and grated

1 small onion, grated

salt and freshly ground black pepper

2 eggs

2 tbsp finely chopped thyme

2 tbsp finely chopped flat-leaf parsley

100g Causeway Castlequarter cheese or other good Cheddar cheese, crumbled

50g plain flour

about 4 tbsp groundnut oil for frying

SERVES 4

Place the potatoes and onion in a colander over a bowl or plate and sprinkle with a pinch of salt. Allow to drain for 20–30 minutes. Put the potatoes and onion in a clean tea towel and squeeze out any excess liquid.

In a large mixing bowl, lightly beat the eggs and mix in the potatoes and onions, thyme, parsley, cheese, flour, salt and pepper.

Heat half the oil in a frying pan until hot but not smoking. Place four 8cm straight-sided scone cutters in the pan. Spoon some of the pancake mixture into each one, to a depth of about 1cm and press down. Cook over gentle heat for about 5 minutes until golden brown underneath.

Remove the cutters and turn the pancakes, then cook until they are golden brown on the other side. Transfer the cooked pancakes to a warm plate and keep warm.

Repeat the process to make another 4 pancakes, adding more oil to the pan if necessary. Serve immediately.

Fried Banana and Maple Syrup on Toast

Not an obviously healthy breakfast, but it does contain one of your five a day! It's maybe a little rich, but it certainly starts the day with a kick.

1 ripe banana

olive oil for frying

knob of butter, plus extra for spreading

juice of ½ lemon

1 tsp brown sugar

1 thick slice white bread or treacle bread, toasted

generous drizzle of maple syrup

SERVES 1

Cut the banana in half lengthways, and then cut each length in half again. Heat a frying pan over medium heat and add a little olive oil and the butter.

When the butter begins to froth, add the banana. Cook, turning occasionally, until the banana is brown on all sides. Pour over the lemon juice, add the sugar and continue to cook, turning the pieces all the time, for a further minute.

Butter the toast liberally, arrange the banana on top and drizzle over that all-important maple syrup.

French Toast, Bacon and Maple Syrup

This is one of my favourite breakfasts for late Sunday morning. Late because we've probably been working the night before, and late because it's Sunday, and that's what Sundays are all about: relaxing, enjoying a big breakfast, watching *Countryfile*, pottering in the garden and thinking about what to have for dinner.

olive oil for frying

8 dry-cure bacon rashers

2 eggs

splash of milk

4 slices plain white bread

maple syrup, to taste

SERVES 4

Preheat the oven to 150°C, ready for keeping the bacon warm while you are cooking the French toast.

Heat a frying pan and add a little olive oil. Fry the bacon until it is crisp and then transfer it to a baking tray. Place in the oven to keep warm. Leave the frying pan over medium heat.

Whisk the eggs and milk together in a large shallow bowl. Dip both sides of each slice of bread in the egg mixture then add them to the pan. Cook over medium heat until golden brown on both sides. You will probably have to cook the French toast in batches, so keep the cooked slices warm in the oven until the others are ready.

When all the French toast is cooked, serve it with the bacon and pour over as much maple syrup as you like.

Strawberry Jam

I like my jam with some texture and when the strawberries are good, it is best not to pulverise them completely. Work gently with the strawberries and you're guaranteed to have jam with a wonderful consistency. To sterilise jam jars, wash them in hot, soapy water and rinse thoroughly. Preheat the oven to 190ºC. Stand them on a folded tea towel in a roasting tin and place in the oven for about 15 minutes. If you pour hot jam into hot jars, there's much less risk of the jars cracking.

1.8kg strawberries (not over-ripe)
1.4kg preserving sugar
50ml lemon juice
good knob of butter

MAKES ABOUT 3KG

Hull the strawberries and give them a quick wipe with kitchen paper (they may become waterlogged or bruised if you wash them). Place a layer of strawberries into a preserving pan, followed by a layer of sugar, and repeat until all the sugar and strawberries are used up. Cover and leave the sugar to draw the liquid from the strawberries for at least 4 hours or, preferably, overnight.

Add the lemon juice to the preserving pan and heat over low to medium heat, stirring gently or simply shaking the pan from time to time, until the sugar has dissolved. Place three or four saucers in the freezer at this point.

Once the sugar has dissolved completely, turn up the heat and boil the jam for 15–20 minutes. Check whether the jam is ready and has reached setting point by putting a small spoonful on one of the frozen saucers. When the jam cools a little, it should form a skin that wrinkles when pushed with one finger. If it does not form a skin, boil the jam for another few minutes and test again.

When the jam is ready, remove it from the heat, skim any scum off the top and gently stir in the butter. Pour the jam into sterilised jam jars. Cover with greaseproof paper discs and allow to cool completely before sealing and labelling.

Rose Petal Jam

This is an unusual recipe that I hadn't used for years, because I haven't had a garden until recently. Use your own roses or those of family and friends so you know that they haven't been sprayed with any chemicals.

350g rose petals from flowers in full bloom

700g preserving sugar

1.7 litres water

juice of 4 large lemons

MAKES ABOUT 2.2KG

Using scissors, remove and discard the white part at the base of each petal. Place the petals in a roasting tin or ovenproof casserole. Sprinkle with half the sugar, cover and leave to stand overnight. This process will extract colour and flavour from the petals.

Put three or four saucers in the freezer. Pour the water, lemon juice and remaining sugar into a preserving pan and heat gently to dissolve the sugar. Do not allow the mixture to boil. Once the sugar has dissolved, add the petals and sugar mixture and stir well to ensure that the new addition of sugar dissolves too.

Turn up the heat and boil the mixture for about 20 minutes, until the jam has thickened slightly. Check whether the jam is ready by putting a small spoonful onto one of the frozen saucers. When the jam cools a little, it should form a skin. If it does not begin to set, boil the jam for another few minutes and test again.

When the jam is ready, remove it from the heat, skim any scum off the top and pour it into sterilised jam jars (see opposite). Cover with greaseproof paper discs and allow to cool completely before sealing and labelling.

Raspberry and White Chocolate Muffins

Muffins are so easy – I can't believe more people don't make them at home. The first muffin should be ready to try within half an hour of beginning your baking session. I bet you can't resist eating them before they are completely cool!

200g plain flour

½ tsp bicarbonate of soda

2 tsp baking powder

80g caster sugar

1 egg

200ml buttermilk

80g butter, melted

125g raspberries (fresh or frozen)

100g good quality white chocolate, roughly chopped

MAKES 10

Preheat the oven to 200°C. Line a muffin tin with 10 muffin cases.

Start with the dry ingredients: sift the flour, bicarbonate of soda and baking powder into a large bowl. Add the caster sugar and mix.

In a separate bowl, beat the egg then stir in the buttermilk and melted butter. Add the egg mixture to the dry ingredients and mix gently with a spatula. Do not overwork – the secret of lovely light muffins is to be gentle. Fold in the raspberries and white chocolate.

Pour the mixture into the cases and bake for 20 minutes, until the muffins are pale golden, risen, cracked on top and springy to the touch. Remove from the oven and cool on a wire rack.

Bloody Mary

Somehow its spicy, meaty quality makes Bloody Mary the ideal drink for brunch and perfectly acceptable at 11 a.m. Although it's a classic, everyone will have their own slightly different version. I like mine punchy, with plenty of heat, but you can easily tone down the flavour by leaving out the horseradish. Absolut black pepper vodka and Big Tom spiced tomato juice make the best Bloody Marys.

ice cubes

100ml vodka

300ml tomato juice

dash of Worcestershire sauce

dash of Tabasco sauce

juice of 1 lime

1 tsp horseradish sauce (optional)

60ml manzanilla dry sherry (optional)

2 celery sticks

SERVES 2

Put some ice cubes into the bottom of a jug. Add the vodka, tomato juice, Worcestershire sauce, Tabasco, lime juice, horseradish sauce and sherry, and mix well. Pour into two highball glasses and serve with sticks of celery.

Late Night Breakfast: The Bean, Bacon, Egg and Whatever-is-in-the-Fridge Baked Fry

For me, the late-night breakfast is usually a spontaneous meal driven by hunger and the need for some soakage to reverse the effects of the last few ill-advised 'ones for the road'. Here is a very tasty, not-quite-haute-cuisine, recipe that hits the spot. If you don't have sausages and bacon, then use any other suitable ingredients that are lurking in the fridge. This is a very flexible recipe – as flexible as you may be at this time of night . . .

4–6 sausages

olive oil for cooking

3–4 dry-cure bacon rashers

2 x 415g cans baked beans

freshly ground black pepper

chilli powder to taste

6 eggs

100g brie or Cheddar cheese, thinly sliced

lots of buttered toast to serve

SERVES 4–6 HUNGRY REVELLERS

Preheat the oven to 190ºC.

Place the sausages in a roasting tin with a little olive oil and fry on the hob, turning the sausages occasionally, until they are lightly cooked. Remove the sausages and fry the bacon in the same tin.

Cut the sausages into quarters and return them to the tin with the bacon. Pour in the beans and season well with the pepper and chilli, to taste.

Bake the mixture for 10 minutes. Remove the tin from the oven and make six depressions in the beans with the back of a spoon. Crack an egg into each hollow and top with the cheese. Return the tin to the oven and bake for a further 10 minutes. This allows some time to assemble a mountain of toast.

Dive in as soon as the baked fry is ready – before it's all gone. Then it will definitely be time to find a comfortable couch.

Deli Favour-ites

Houmous / Tapenade / Sun-blushed Tomato Tapenade / Simple, Crusty, Staple-of-Life Bread / Focaccia / Ciabatta / Pan Bagnat / Panzanella / Aïoli / Mayonnaise / Celeriac Remoulade / Aubergine and Tomato Salad / Spiced Potato and Chorizo Salad / Saffron Couscous with Roasted Peppers, Toasted Almonds and Coriander / Mushroom and Parmesan Puffs with Truffle Oil / Duck Confit Pie with Cranberries / Thai Fish Cakes / Scones / Chocolate Brownies / Chilli Hot Chocolate / Coconut and Passionfruit Slices

Houmous

The key to these delicious dips is freshness, so when you are preparing this recipe or its variations, or the tapenade opposite, only make enough for that day. I know the stuff will keep for days but it won't have the punch it did when you first prepared it. Serve with some toasted sourdough or hot flat bread.

2 x 400g cans chickpeas, drained

1 garlic clove, chopped

3 tbsp tahini

juice of 1 lemon

100ml extra-virgin olive oil

salt and freshly ground black pepper

SERVES 6–8

Place the chickpeas, garlic, tahini, lemon juice, olive oil and seasoning in a food processor. Blitz, scraping down the contents of the bowl once or twice so that the mixture purées evenly, until the houmous is as smooth in texture as you like.

Variations

Sweet Chilli Houmous

Simply add a couple of dessertspoons of sweet chilli sauce to give your dip a little kick.

Thai Green Curry Houmous

For a slightly higher-octane dip, add a teaspoon of Thai green curry paste, a squeeze of lime juice and a bunch of chopped coriander.

Tapenade

150g pitted black olives

2 garlic cloves, chopped

15g drained capers

2 anchovy fillets

1 tbsp chopped flat-leaf parsley

leaves from 4 thyme sprigs

juice of ½ lemon

freshly ground black pepper

4 tbsp olive oil

SERVES 4–6

Blitz all the ingredients, except the olive oil, in a food processor until evenly chopped but not too fine. With the motor running, gradually add the olive oil until the tapenade is at the consistency you like. I prefer a rough texture, so I don't over-process the ingredients.

Sun-blushed Tomato Tapenade

150g drained sun-blushed tomatoes (reserve the oil)

25g pine nuts, toasted

juice of ½ lemon

25g fresh Parmesan cheese, grated

1 garlic clove, chopped

salt and freshly ground black pepper

5 tbsp olive oil, drained from the tomatoes

SERVES 4–6

Blitz all the ingredients, except the olive oil, in a food processor. Add olive oil until the tapenade is at the consistency you like. I prefer a rough texture, so I don't over-blitz the ingredients.

Bread

Baking bread is not an exact science. All sorts of things affect the end result: the temperature of your kitchen, the humidity, the yeast, the flour … in fact, almost everything you can think of has a slight bearing on how your loaf will turn out. Maybe even your state of mind influences the final result.

However, there is something that feels inherently good about being able to produce such a staple of life. Maybe it is the very hands-on method of production, the smell of bread in the oven, or even the feeling of satisfaction when you cut into that crisp crust.

Mastering the art of baking bread is hugely satisfying – knowing that a loaf is going to turn out just right by the way it feels in your hand and by the look of it as it disappears into the oven.

I have tried to keep things as simple as possible in this section. As a chef, knowing which flavours go well together, I always find experimenting very satisfying. As you practise and become more confident, you can experiment with different flours, new flavours and toppings – but first, the basics.

Simple, Crusty, Staple-of-Life Bread

We always use fresh yeast for our breads at The Yellow Door. You can buy fresh yeast from us, home bakeries, the bakery departments of some supermarkets – any establishment that makes its own bread.

1kg strong white flour

20g salt

20g fresh yeast

700ml lukewarm water (at blood temperature)

extra flour or semolina, for dusting

MAKES 2 LOAVES

Place the flour in the biggest mixing bowl you have. Add the salt and crumble in the yeast, keeping them on separate sides of the bowl. The salt will destroy some of the effectiveness of the yeast if they come into direct contact at this point. Add most of the water and mix with a wooden spoon for 2 minutes to form a sticky but spongy dough.

If the dough looks a little dry, add the rest of the water and mix for a further minute. If the consistency looks right, flour the dough liberally and turn it out onto a floured surface. Using your hands, tuck the sides of the dough under to form a tight ball.

Knead the dough by pushing it away from you with the palms of your hands and then folding it up again. Continue kneading for 10 minutes, working firmly but gently. After kneading, the dough should be firm, spongy and elastic in texture. Place the dough back in the bowl and cover it with a damp, clean tea towel. Place the dough somewhere warm but not too hot to prove. The dough should double in size in 45–60 minutes. Do not be tempted to proceed until the dough has risen properly.

Turn the dough out onto a floured surface, scraping out any that has stuck to the side of the bowl and adding it to the rest. Knock back the dough by dimpling it with your fingertips and then knead it for another minute or so. To shape your loaves, tuck the dough into two tight balls, place them on baking trays and sprinkle with a little flour or semolina. Cover with a clean, damp tea towel. Allow to prove again for another 45 minutes until the loaves have doubled in size once more.

Simple, Crusty, Staple-of-Life Bread (. . . cont.)

Preheat the oven to 240°C. Sprinkle the bread with flour or semolina and place it very gently in the oven. Do not knock the trays as this will cause the dough to fall. Quickly splash about ¼ cup (about 50–60ml) of water onto the base of the oven and immediately close the door, without slamming it. This water will turn to steam and give your bread a wonderful crisp crust. Bake the bread for 10–15 minutes. Don't open the door to peek during this first cooking period as the steam will escape.

Reduce the oven temperature to 220°C and bake the bread for a further 30 minutes. To check if the bread is cooked, turn it over and tap it on the base. If it sounds hollow, it is ready; if not, return it to the oven for a further 5 minutes. Cool the bread on a wire rack.

Don't be tempted to cut your first slice from the loaf until it is almost completely cooled. Easy to say but hard to do as that evocative smell drifts through your kitchen.

Focaccia

One of our most popular breads. The volume of olive oil added to the dough during preparation and at the end of cooking may seem excessive, but this is entirely correct and gives the bread its distinctive flavour, moisture and character, and helps to give it a longer shelf life.

You will notice that I use ferment (sometimes called sponge dough) in this recipe. We never use any unnatural additives or yeast enhancers in any of our bread. Instead we use ferment: a natural, traditional method that adds flavour and texture and gives our bread a kick. Ferment is simply one-day-old dough that has been allowed to prove once, knocked back and then stored in a sealed container in the fridge. You can use the Simple, Crusty, Staple-of-Life Bread recipe (pages 25–6) for this purpose.

100g ferment

450g strong unbleached flour

½ tsp salt

20g fresh yeast

75ml olive oil, plus extra for brushing

25ml champagne vinegar

260ml lukewarm water (at blood temperature)

2 tsp rock salt

MAKES 1 LOAF

Prepare the ferment 24 hours in advance to allow time for it to prove. Knock back, cover and chill.

Brush a large bowl or plastic bucket with olive oil. The dough will double in volume, so the bowl or bucket must be large enough to accommodate this.

Place the ferment, flour, salt, yeast, 25ml of the olive oil, the champagne vinegar and water in a mixer fitted with a dough hook, taking care not to place the yeast and salt in direct contact. Mix on low speed for 3 minutes. Set the mixer to medium speed and mix for a further 4 minutes. The dough should be quite soft. Add more water if necessary.

As the dough is mixed, it should form one ball, thrown around the bowl by the mixer. With your finger on the stop button of the mixer, throw a small handful of flour onto the inside of the bowl and turn the mixer off immediately. Turn out the dough into the oiled container – it will come out in one ball. Scrape the dough hook clean by hand and add this extra dough to the dough in the oiled container. Cover the container with clingfilm and place in a warm spot until the dough has doubled in size, which will take about 45 minutes.

Focaccia (... cont.)

Preheat the oven to 220°C.

Meanwhile, generously oil a Swiss roll tin or oven tray, measuring approximately 28 x 23cm. When the dough has doubled in size, turn it out onto the tray or tin and, using your hands, flatten the dough evenly over the tray, pressing it right into the corners. The dough will be quite elastic, so persevere.

When the bread is spread in a flat layer pour the remaining olive oil over the dough and, using your fingers as if you were playing the piano, dimple the surface of the dough. The olive oil will settle into little pools in the hollows. Sprinkle with rock salt. Once again allow the dough to prove in a warm place until doubled in size, which will again take about 45 minutes.

Have ¼ cup (about 50–60ml) of water ready when you put the focaccia in the oven. Quickly throw the water into the oven before you shut the door (do not slam the door). Be careful of the steam. Cook the foccacia for 35–40 minutes until golden and fully baked. Remove from the oven and brush liberally with more olive oil, then allow to cool before cutting.

Variations

Rosemary and Red Onion Focaccia
Simply add 1 finely sliced red onion and the chopped leaves from a couple of sprigs of rosemary to the surface of the focaccia before its second proving.

My favourite: Goat's Cheese and Roasted Pepper Focaccia
Scatter good goat's cheese, crumbled, and diced roasted peppers over the focaccia before the second proving.

Ciabatta

500g ferment (see page 27)

500g strong unbleached flour

10g salt

15g fresh yeast

50ml milk

50ml olive oil

280ml lukewarm water (at blood temperature)

olive oil, for brushing

extra flour, for dusting

MAKES 4 LOAVES

Prepare the ferment 24 hours in advance. Knock back, cover and chill.

Brush a large bowl or plastic bucket with olive oil. The dough will double in volume, so the container must be large enough to accommodate it.

Place the flour and salt in a food mixer. Add the yeast, keeping it well away from the salt at this stage. Pour in the milk, olive oil and most of the water. Using the dough hook, mix on low speed for 3 minutes until the dough has come together into a soft ball. Add a little more water if necessary. Once you have made this recipe a few times you will begin to know the feel of a really good dough ball that will bake into nice bread. Add the ferment and mix for a further 5 minutes on medium-high speed until the dough is smooth and elastic.

As the dough is mixed, it should form one ball, thrown around the bowl by the mixer. With your finger on the stop button of the mixer, throw a small handful of flour onto the inside of the bowl and turn the mixer off immediately. Turn out the dough into the oiled container – it will come out in one ball. Scrape the dough hook clean by hand and add this extra dough to the dough in the container. Cover the container with clingfilm and place in a warm spot until the dough has doubled in size, which will take about 45 minutes.

Turn the dough out onto a lightly floured surface. Dust some flour over the top of the dough, then stretch it into a square. Cut the dough into fingers about 10cm wide – you should get about four fingers out of this quantity. Using your hands like two shovels, push them under both ends of each finger of dough and lift the dough onto a lightly floured baking sheet, stretching it slightly as you go. Repeat with the remaining fingers of dough.

Cover the baking sheets with a slightly damp, clean tea towel. Leave them in a warm place until doubled in size, which will again take about 45 minutes.

Preheat the oven to 245°C. Dust the ciabatta loaves lightly with flour and bake for 20–22 minutes.

Variations

Sun-dried Tomato Ciabatta
Reduce the water by 20ml. Drain 75g chopped sun-dried tomatoes of their oil, chop them and add with the other ingredients before mixing the dough.

Cheese and Onion Ciabatta
Add 1 finely chopped onion and 75g grated mature Cheddar cheese towards the end of the second high-speed mixing.

Olive Ciabatta
Add 60g pitted olives towards the end of the second high-speed mixing.

Parmesan Ciabatta
Add 75g grated Parmesan cheese to the dough before the first mixing. Instead of dusting with flour before baking, sprinkle a further 60g finely grated Parmesan over the loaves.

Pan Bagnat

This is a classic French recipe with its origins in peasant field food. It's absolutely brilliant for a picnic as you can make it the night before and keep it overnight in the fridge where the flavours develop, and the origins of the name – meaning 'wet bread' – become apparent. It's even great for kids' lunchboxes.

1 red pepper

200g broad beans, shelled

6 large ripe tomatoes

4 drained, canned or bottled artichoke hearts, sliced

1 shallot, finely sliced

1 ciabatta loaf

1 garlic clove

1 tbsp red wine vinegar

drizzle of extra-virgin olive oil

200g can tuna, drained (use good quality tuna)

2 eggs, soft-boiled, peeled and sliced

8 good quality anchovy fillets

small handful of pitted black olives

handful of basil leaves

SERVES 4

Preheat the grill. Halve the pepper and discard the seeds, then place skin-side up under the grill. When the skin is blistered and blackened, put the pepper halves in a bowl and cover with clingfilm. When cool enough to handle, peel off the skin and slice the flesh.

Cook the broad beans in boiling salted water for about 5 minutes. Drain and immediately plunge them into cold water. Drain again and remove the skins from the beans.

Blanch the tomatoes in a pan of boiling water for 10–15 seconds, then place them straight into a bowl of iced water. Remove from the water, peel the tomatoes, then halve them, discard the seeds and slice. Mix the beans, tomatoes, pepper, artichoke hearts and shallot.

Slice the ciabatta loaf in half horizontally and scoop out about two-thirds of the bread from inside both halves. Rub the inside with garlic and drizzle with the vinegar and olive oil. Pile an even layer of the mixed vegetables on half of the ciabatta.

Evenly distribute the tuna, eggs, anchovies and olives over the vegetables. Tear up the basil leaves and scatter them over the top. Place the other half of the loaf on top and wrap tightly in foil. Put the loaf on a chopping board and place another board or roasting tin on top. Weigh down the board or tin and leave overnight in the fridge. Bring to room temperature before serving.

Panzanella

1 ciabatta loaf, preferably 2–3 days old

500g ripe tomatoes, preferably plum tomatoes

2 garlic cloves, crushed

salt and freshly ground black pepper

150ml extra-virgin olive oil, plus extra for drizzling

2 tbsp red wine vinegar

1 red pepper

1 yellow pepper

1 red onion

½ cucumber, peeled, halved lengthways and deseeded

50g good quality anchovy fillets

large bunch of basil leaves

50g capers, drained

1 red chilli, thinly sliced (remove the seeds for less heat)

SERVES 6

Cut the ciabatta lengthways down the middle and then across about every 4cm to give big chunks of bread. If the bread is fresh, preheat the oven to 100°C and dry out the bread in the oven for about 40 minutes. Make sure you don't forget about the bread and brown or burn the pieces! Place the bread in a bowl.

Blanch the tomatoes in batches in a pan of boiling water for 10–15 seconds, then place them straight into a bowl of iced water. Drain and peel the tomatoes, then quarter and deseed them over a sieve over a bowl. As you quarter the tomatoes, the juices will gather in the bowl under the sieve. Reserve these juices. Place the tomato quarters in a separate bowl and discard the seeds.

Add the garlic, salt and pepper, olive oil and red wine vinegar to the reserved tomato juices. Stir well, then pour over the bread and set aside.

Preheat the grill. Cut the peppers in half, discard their seeds and place skin-side up under the grill. When the skin is blistered and blackened, put the pepper halves in a bowl. Cover with clingfilm until cool enough to handle, then peel off the skin. Cut the peppers into large chunks. Cut the onion and cucumber into similar-sized large chunks. Cut each anchovy fillet into three. Tear up the basil leaves.

In a large salad bowl, carefully mix all the ingredients, including the bread. Cover and leave at room temperature for at least 30 minutes. Just before serving, add a good drizzle of olive oil and stir gently.

Aïoli

Traditionally you only use egg yolks to make aïoli but when cooking at home, I usually use a whole egg as it makes the mixture more stable and less likely to curdle. If you do not have a large pestle and mortar, crush the garlic and salt together, then place in a blender, or bowl (if using a hand-held blender), or use a food processor. Aïoli keeps well in the fridge for up to a week.

2 garlic cloves
pinch of Maldon sea salt
juice of ½ lemon
1 egg
450ml extra-virgin olive oil

MAKES APPROXIMATELY 500ML

Crush the garlic and sea salt to a purée in a large mortar. Add the lemon juice and egg. I use a hand-held blender to process the egg in the mortar, with a tea towel to protect me from the splashes. Add the olive oil in a very fine stream, keeping the blender running all the time. Add the oil very slowly at first, taking care not to curdle the aïoli. When all the oil is incorporated, check the seasoning and acidity levels – you may want to add more salt and lemon juice.

Variations

The aïoli can be flavoured with additional ingredients, such as chopped fresh coriander leaves, 3 tbsp saffron-infused water, stirred in at the end of mixing, or by using lime juice instead of the lemon juice and adding the finely grated zest of 1 lime. For a fiery aïoli, add a deseeded and finely-diced chilli or 1 tsp harissa.

Mayonnaise

1 egg yolk
1 tsp Dijon mustard
pinch of salt
small pinch of white pepper
1 tbsp lemon juice
140ml mild olive oil or pure corn oil

MAKES APPROXIMATELY 150ML

Place the egg yolk, mustard, seasoning and lemon juice in a bowl and blend with a whisk or stick blender. Slowly add the oil in a very fine stream, continually whisking or blending until the mixture is thick and creamy.

Celeriac Remoulade

This winter salad is the ideal accompaniment for cold cooked beef, pork and ham, or game pie. I sometimes serve it with grilled or hot-smoked salmon as a simple first course.

1 celeriac, peeled and cut into fine julienne strips

Dressing

2 shallots, finely sliced

2 tbsp chopped mixed herbs, such as flat-leaf parsley, tarragon and chervil

3 tbsp Mayonnaise (see opposite)

2 tbsp crème fraîche

2 tsp Dijon mustard

juice of ½ lemon

salt and freshly ground black pepper

SERVES 6

Mix all the dressing ingredients in a bowl, adding seasoning to taste.

In a separate bowl, mix the celeriac with three-quarters of the dressing. The strips of celeriac should be well coated, creamy but not sloppy. Add more dressing if necessary.

Cover and leave the remoulade for a few hours for the flavours to develop before serving at room temperature.

Aubergine and Tomato Salad

This delicious and refreshing salad is perfect on a summer day. Enjoy it on its own, or use it to accompany barbecued mackerel or sardines. The smokiness of the aubergine complements the barbecue flavour of grilled meats really well, while the acidity of the limes and sharpness of the pomegranate cut the richness of the fat. Grill the aubergine slices over the barbecue coals to enhance the smoky flavour but keep an eye out to ensure that they don't char too quickly and become bitter.

2 aubergines

juice of ½ lemon

salt and freshly ground black pepper

50ml extra-virgin olive oil

5 spring onions, finely chopped

5 ripe tomatoes, deseeded and chopped

3–4 tbsp chopped flat-leaf parsley

2–3 tbsp finely chopped mint leaves

seeds of ½ pomegranate

juice of 1 lime

2 cloves garlic, finely chopped

SERVES 6–8 AS A SIDE DISH,
3–4 AS A MAIN COURSE

Cut the aubergines lengthways into 2cm thick slices. Discard the outer slices as you want exposed flesh on both sides. Place the aubergine in a colander, sprinkle with the lemon juice and liberally with salt, then leave over a bowl for 30 minutes to degorge. This removes any bitter taste from the aubergines. Rinse in cold water and dry thoroughly with a clean tea towel.

Preheat the grill to medium or heat up a griddle pan over medium heat. Brush the aubergine slices lightly with olive oil and season with salt and pepper. Cook for 5 minutes on each side until lightly browned. You may have to do this in batches. Leave to cool.

Cut the aubergine slices into bite-sized pieces and place them in a large salad bowl. Add all the other ingredients, and mix thoroughly but gently. Check for seasoning and serve immediately.

Spiced Potato and Chorizo Salad

This simple, Spanish-style potato salad is great served warm, especially as a light lunch. I sometimes add diced vine tomatoes at the same time as the coriander.

20 baby potatoes, quartered

olive oil, for cooking

2 raw chorizo sausages, for cooking, diced

1 onion, finely sliced

2 garlic cloves, finely chopped

juice of 1 lemon

handful of coriander leaves, chopped

extra-virgin olive oil to dress the salad

salt and freshly ground black pepper

SERVES 4

Cook the baby potatoes in boiling salted water for 12–15 minutes or until tender.

Meanwhile, heat a sauté pan over medium heat and add a splash of olive oil. When hot, add the chorizo and onion. The chorizo will release lots of juices and colour the onion. Fry until the chorizo is cooked and the onion is softened. Then add the garlic, cook for a further minute and remove from the heat.

Drain the potatoes and return them to their pan to dry out over low heat for about 5 minutes.

Place the potatoes in a bowl and add the chorizo, onion and garlic with all the pan juices. Mix gently with a spatula. Add the lemon juice, coriander and a little extra-virgin olive oil, if necessary. Season to taste. Serve immediately.

Saffron Couscous with Roasted Peppers, Toasted Almonds and Coriander

In this recipe, I use a cup to measure the two key ingredients, stock and couscous equally by volume. It doesn't matter too much what size the cup is – a standard teacup is good. When I measure them this way, I always get light fluffy couscous – perfect for serving as an accompaniment or in a salad.

2 red peppers

50g flaked almonds

2 cups vegetable stock

good pinch of saffron threads

2 cups couscous

large bunch of coriander leaves, chopped

salt and freshly ground white pepper

3 tbsp extra-virgin olive oil

juice of 1 lemon

SERVES 6

Preheat the grill. Cut the peppers in half, remove their seeds and place skin-side up under the grill. When the skin is blistered and blackened, put the pepper halves in a bowl and cover with clingfilm. Leave until cool enough to handle, then peel off the skin. Cut the peppers into pieces about the size of a stamp.

Heat a frying pan over medium heat. Add the almonds to the hot dry pan and toast until golden. Watch them carefully, shaking the pan and turning the almonds, as they burn easily.

Bring the vegetable stock and saffron threads to the boil in a pan. Allow to simmer for a couple of minutes and then remove from the heat. Place the couscous in a large heatproof bowl and pour over the hot stock. Stir just once, then immediately cover the bowl with clingfilm. After about 10 minutes, the couscous will have absorbed all the stock and doubled in volume.

Using a whisk, move the couscous around the bowl to separate the grains and fluff it up. Add the peppers, almonds, coriander, seasoning, olive oil and lemon juice. Mix well, check the seasoning and serve.

Mushroom and Parmesan Puffs with Truffle Oil

These puffs are a delicious, indulgent snack, and they'll fill your house with the unmistakable smell of truffle oil while cooking.

olive oil for cooking

1 onion, finely sliced

1kg large flat-cap mushrooms, sliced

2 garlic cloves, finely chopped

250ml double cream

100g Parmesan cheese, grated

handful of flat-leaf parsley, chopped

salt and freshly ground black pepper

1 dsp truffle oil

4 sheets of ready-rolled puff pastry (there are usually 2 sheets in a 425g packet)

1 egg, beaten, to seal

1 egg yolk, beaten, to glaze

MAKES 16

Heat around a tablespoon of oil in a large saucepan. Add the onion and cook over high heat for about 2 minutes or until the onions are starting to colour.

Add half the mushrooms and cook, stirring frequently, until they have reduced in volume by half. Add the remaining mushrooms and continue to cook for a further 5 minutes.

Stir in the garlic and cream and bring the mixture to the boil, then boil vigorously for a few minutes to reduce and thicken the cream. Remove from the heat and stir in the cheese and parsley. Taste, season as necessary and add the truffle oil. Allow the mixture to cool completely before preparing the puffs.

Preheat the oven to 200°C.

Lay the sheets of puff pastry on a lightly floured work surface. Cut each sheet into 4 squares. Place a good spoonful of the mushroom mixture in the middle of each pastry square. Brush the edges with beaten egg, then fold the sides up to meet over the filling and pinch the edges to seal them. Brush the top of each puff with egg yolk to glaze, and cut a small hole in the top to allow hot air to escape during cooking. Place on baking sheets.

Bake for 20–25 minutes, until the pastry is puffed and golden brown. A little mixture might bubble out of the puffs during cooking, but this doesn't matter. Serve immediately.

Duck Confit Pie with Cranberries

Pastry

300g plain flour

pinch of salt

75g butter

75g lard or white vegetable fat

2 egg yolks

olive oil for cooking

6–8 shallots, peeled and finely sliced

2 garlic cloves, finely chopped

1 red apple, peeled, cored and diced

3 tbsp fresh or frozen cranberries

1 glass red wine

small rosemary sprig

small thyme sprig

1 bay leaf

salt and freshly ground black pepper

1 tbsp redcurrant jelly

500ml chicken stock

2 legs duck confit (page 110), skin and bones removed, cut into chunks

1 egg yolk, beaten

SERVES 4–6

To make the pastry, sift the flour and salt into a bowl. Using your fingertips, rub in the butter and lard or white fat until the mixture resembles fine breadcrumbs. Add the egg yolks and about 2 tsp of cold water and mix well until the mixture begins to form clumps. Bring the mixture together into a ball using your hand. Wrap in clingfilm and chill for at least 1 hour.

Heat a little oil in a pan over medium heat. Add the shallots and sauté until they are golden brown. Add the garlic, apple and cranberries and continue to cook for a further 2 minutes. Add the red wine, rosemary, thyme, bay leaf and seasoning and bring to the boil. Simmer until the wine has reduced by two-thirds. Next stir in the stock and redcurrant jelly and bring to the boil again. Cook until the cranberries and apples have softened and the mixture resembles loose chutney. Set aside to cool.

Preheat the oven to 180°C.

Lightly grease a 20cm loose-bottomed pie dish. Roll out two-thirds of the pastry and use it to line the dish. Pour in the shallot mixture and place the duck pieces on top. Roll out the remaining third of pastry to form a lid. Brush the edges of the pie with water and place the lid on top. Crimp with a fork or your finger and thumb to seal the edge. Cut a small whole in the top to allow steam to escape. Finally brush the top of the pie with egg yolk and bake for 35–40 minutes until the pie is golden brown. Serve with a crisp salad.

Thai Fish Cakes

This unconventional recipe started out as a simple salmon and potato cake to use up salmon tails, but it morphed into this spicier Thai version. It has been a Yellow Door staple, both on the deli counter and on our lunchtime menu, for some years, and is still one of my favourites. This recipe makes a large quantity but it is as easy to make fifteen cakes as five or six, and they freeze well. Japanese breadcrumbs can be difficult to find but they are available in specialist food shops and some supermarkets.

300g salmon, skinned

300g undyed smoked haddock, skinned

150ml single cream

4 red chillies, deseeded and finely diced

8cm fresh root ginger, peeled and finely grated

4 garlic cloves, finely chopped

2 lemongrass stalks (white parts only), very finely chopped

650g potatoes, boiled and mashed

100g peeled cooked prawns, roughly chopped

1 tbsp fish sauce

1 tsp light soy sauce

1 tsp sesame oil

good handful of coriander leaves, chopped

grated zest of 2 limes

salt and freshly ground white pepper

50g plain flour, plus extra for dusting

2 eggs

100ml milk

125g Japanese breadcrumbs, or other dry breadcrumbs

1 tbsp sesame seeds

1 tbsp desiccated coconut

MAKES ABOUT 15

Preheat the oven to 170°C.

Place the salmon and haddock in an ovenproof dish. Pour over the cream, cover tightly with foil and bake for 15–20 minutes, until the fish is cooked. Drain the fish in a sieve over a saucepan. Place the saucepan on high heat and boil the creamy cooking juices until reduced by three-quarters. Now add the chillies, ginger, garlic and lemongrass and remove from the heat.

Place the mashed potato in a large bowl. Add the prawns, warm creamy cooking juices, fish sauce, soy sauce, sesame oil, coriander and lime zest. Mix well. Flake the fish into the bowl by hand, removing all bones. Mix gently without breaking up the fish too much. Season to taste. Add a tablespoonful of breadcrumbs if the mixture is too soft.

Turn out the mixture onto a floured surface and pat it out to a thickness of 2–3cm. Use a 6cm straight-sided cutter to stamp out cakes. Place them on a baking sheet, cover and chill for about 20 minutes, until just firm.

In the meantime, prepare the coating mixes. Place the flour in a bowl and season it well. Whisk the eggs and milk together. In a third bowl, mix the breadcrumbs, sesame seeds and coconut.

Coat each fishcake in seasoned flour, then egg, then breadcrumbs. At this point you can either freeze the fish cakes, or shallow fry them in 1–2cm of hot oil for 2–3 minutes on each side until they are crisp and golden. Drain well on kitchen paper. Serve with coriander and lime Aïoli (page 34) and salad leaves.

Scones

Here in Northern Ireland, scones are a morning institution. The ones we bake at The Yellow Door are big enough to count for breakfast and a light lunch put together, and are perennially popular.

When making scones, rule number one is that butter is best. We never use any homogenised fats. I could save thousands of pounds by using cheaper margarine but I would rather cut out my tongue. I strongly believe that there is nothing quite like the flavour of Irish butter. So I make no apology for using full-fat, flavoursome butter in all our recipes. It simply is the best. We sell thousands of scones every year, so I believe that I'm right on this one.

The other vital ingredient for good scones is buttermilk. Made with these ingredients and served with more Irish butter and home-made jam, there's nothing better than scones. Who needs pain au chocolat?

Scones

700g soda bread flour

150g caster sugar

½ tsp salt

120g butter

750ml buttermilk

1 egg, beaten

MAKES 20 LARGE SCONES

Preheat the oven to 200°C.

Mix the flour, caster sugar and salt in a bowl. Add the butter and rub it in, using your fingers, until the mixture resembles breadcrumbs. Add the buttermilk and mix again until the mixture starts to come together.

Turn the mixture out onto a lightly floured surface and work it with your hands until it forms a ball. Pat out to a thickness of 4–5cm and, using a large scone cutter, stamp out the scones. Place them on a baking sheet and glaze the tops with beaten egg.

Bake for 20–25 minutes until golden on top and cooked through. Serve warm from the oven with home-made preserves and lots more good Irish butter.

Variations

Mix in any of the following ingredients when the mixture resembles breadcrumbs, before you add the buttermilk:

100g fresh or frozen blueberries
1 red apple, cored and diced, 1 tsp cinnamon
75g fresh or frozen raspberries, 75g chopped
    white chocolate
100g sultanas
1 banana, diced
100g glacé cherries

Chocolate Brownies

This is one of our original secret recipes . . . which I am now disclosing to you. We first made these brownies for ourselves and used them like Red Bull to give us energy before a busy service. The recipe has never changed, even now, when we make thousands of them. A real treat.

280g plain chocolate (at least 60% cocoa solids), broken into pieces

400g unsalted butter, plus extra for greasing

6 eggs

560g caster sugar

90g plain flour

100g walnuts, roughly chopped

MAKES 12

Preheat the oven to 180°C. Line a 25cm square baking tin with greaseproof paper and lightly brush with butter.

Melt the chocolate and butter together in a bowl over a pan of simmering water. Meanwhile, whisk the eggs and sugar together in a large bowl until pale and creamy, either by hand or using a hand-held electric beater.

Add the melted chocolate and butter to the eggs. Sift in the flour and add the walnuts. Then use a spatula to fold everything gently together.

Pour the mixture into the prepared tin and bake for 45–50 minutes. The mixture should still be slightly soft in the centre when the brownies are cooked, so a skewer will not come out clean. Leave to cool completely before cutting into squares.

Chilli Hot Chocolate

A wonderfully warming drink to sip on a winter's day picnic at the beach, as you watch the waves crash onto the shore. I would avoid serving it with the traditional marshmallows. For added spice you can add a couple of cloves, a piece of cinnamon stick or a star anise to the milk at the infusing stage.

1 litre milk

2 red chillies, halved lengthways and deseeded

200g plain chocolate (at least 60% cocoa solids), broken into small pieces

200ml single cream

SERVES 4

Pour the milk into a saucepan. Pop in the chillies and bring to a slow simmer, taking care not to let the milk boil over. Remove from the heat and set aside for 10 minutes to let the chilli infuse.

Add the chocolate and cream, and reheat over low heat. Stir constantly until the chocolate has melted, then remove the chillies. Serve immediately, or pour into a thermos flask for your picnic.

Coconut and Passionfruit Slices

The creamy coconut topping, flavoured with the sharp, acidic and exotic passionfruit turns a tea break into a really great tea break.

Sweet pastry

125g unsalted butter, at room temperature

100g caster sugar

1 large egg

1 tsp vanilla extract

120g plain flour

1 tsp baking powder

salt

Coconut topping

4 large eggs

125g caster sugar

75g plain flour

150g desiccated coconut

300ml double cream

150ml coconut milk

grated zest and juice of 1 lemon

pulp from 6 large passionfruit

icing sugar for dusting

MAKES 18

Preheat the oven to 180°C.

To make the pastry, cream the butter and sugar together until pale and soft. Add the egg and vanilla extract, and beat well. Sift in the flour, baking powder and a pinch of salt to make a sticky dough.

Grease an 18 x 28cm shallow roasting tray and line it with non-stick baking parchment. With floured hands, press the pastry into the tin (good for the kids to do), covering the bottom evenly, and bake for 15 minutes or until the pastry is pale gold in colour.

Make the topping by whisking the eggs and sugar together for about 3 minutes until they are pale and thick. Sift in the flour and add the coconut, cream, coconut milk, lemon zest and juice, and passionfruit pulp. Mix well. Pour the coconut mix over the pastry base and bake for about 40 minutes until the topping is golden and set.

Allow to cool completely in the tin. Cut into 18 squares and dust with icing sugar before serving.

First Courses

Shallot Tart Tatin with Red Wine and Balsamic Vinegar / Fried Baby Squid with Garlic and Lemon / Dublin Bay Prawn and Chive Tart with Prawn and Lemon Mayonnaise / Cashel Blue Tart / Mushroom Soup with Porcini and Herbs / Rich Tomato and Parmesan Soup / Vichyssoise / Roasted Spiced Butternut Squash Soup / Leek, Potato and Bacon Soup / Barbecued Langoustines with Lime, Coriander and Smoked Chilli / Smoked Chicken Fillet / Smoked Eel and Pancetta Salad / Gravad Lax of Salmon / Horseradish Panna Cotta / Irish Whiskey-marinated Smoked Salmon / Soused Lough Neagh Pollen / Little Gem, Pear and Bellingham Blue Salad with Toasted Walnuts / Jilly's Goat's Cheese, Beetroot and Toasted Pine Nut Salad / Paul's Game Terrine / Chicken Liver Pâté / Pan-seared Woodpigeon with Puy Lentils, Lamb's Lettuce and Roasted Walnut Dressing / Pan-seared Foie Gras with Caramelised Apples and Roasted Hazelnut Dressing / Carpaccio of Venison with Pickled Walnuts, Parsley Cress and Horseradish Crème Fraîche / Pan-seared Slow-cooked Pork Belly with Creamed Savoy Cabbage and Whiskey Honey Glaze

Shallot Tart Tatin with Red Wine and Balsamic Vinegar

This dish is an ideal first course or light lunch. Serve with a salad of bitter greens, like frisée, and perhaps some shaved Parmesan.

20 shallots

2 tbsp olive oil

2 garlic cloves, chopped

2 glasses full-bodied red wine

4 tbsp aged balsamic vinegar

1 bay leaf

good pinch of brown sugar

1 rosemary sprig

salt and freshly ground black pepper

1 sheet ready-rolled puff pastry

SERVES 4

Preheat the oven to 190°C.

Peel the shallots, taking care to remove as little of the root end as possible as the roots prevent the shallots from falling apart during cooking.

Heat the olive oil in a large pan over high heat. Add the shallots and cook, stirring regularly, until they are browned and caramelised all over. Add the garlic, red wine, balsamic vinegar, bay leaf, sugar, rosemary and seasoning. Bring to the boil and continue boiling until the wine and vinegar have reduced to a syrupy consistency.

Remove the bay leaf and rosemary, and pour the shallots into a small sauté pan with a metallic handle or suitable baking tin. Alternatively divide the shallots among four individual pans or baking tins. Allow the shallot mixture to cool.

Unroll the puff pastry and cut out one large or four small circles – the pastry should be slightly larger than the pan containing the shallots. Prick the pastry all over with a fork. Place the pastry on top of the pan(s), tucking it in around the rim, and bake for 15 minutes, until the pastry is golden and fully cooked.

Leave the baked tart(s) to rest for 3–4 minutes before turning out on a serving platter or individual plates. Serve immediately.

Fried Baby Squid with Garlic and Lemon

1kg baby squid, well washed and cut into rings and tentacles

olive oil for cooking

salt and freshly ground black pepper

100g butter

juice of 1 large lemon

4 garlic cloves, finely chopped

1 bunch of flat-leaf parsley, chopped

2 handfuls baby rocket leaves

SERVES 4

Place the squid in a bowl with a splash of olive oil. Season lightly. Heat a griddle or frying pan over high heat. Add the squid in a single layer – you may need to cook it in two batches – and cook for no longer than 1 minute on each side. It will colour quickly. When cooked, place on a warm plate.

Heat another frying pan over medium heat. When hot, add the butter and allow to melt and froth, followed by the lemon juice and garlic. Cook for a minute before mixing in the squid, parsley and seasoning, to taste.

Divide the rocket among four plates. Spoon over the squid and dressing and serve immediately.

Dublin Bay Prawn and Chive Tart with Prawn and Lemon Mayonnaise

I love freshly-baked savoury tarts served with a little herb salad. This dish is very versatile and can be proudly served as a first course at a dinner party or for a summer afternoon get-together with friends. Crack open a bottle of champagne or cava to accompany it.

Pastry

200g plain flour plus extra for dusting

pinch of salt

50g butter

50g lard or white vegetable fat

1 egg yolk

Filling

30 raw Dublin Bay prawns

3 eggs

125ml milk

125ml cream

1 tbsp finely chopped chives

salt and freshly ground black pepper

Mayonnaise

1 shallot, finely chopped

olive oil for cooking

prawn shells and juices

1 bay leaf

3–4 parsley stalks

glass of white wine

3 tbsp Mayonnaise (page 34)

juice of ½ lemon

soft-leafed herbs to garnish, such as flat-leaf parsley, chives, dill, fennel or basil

SERVES 4

To make the pastry, sift the flour and salt into a bowl. Using your fingertips, rub in the butter and lard or white fat until the mixture resembles fine breadcrumbs. Add the egg yolk and about 2 tsp of cold water and mix well until the mixture begins to form clumps. Bring the mixture together into a ball using your hand. Wrap in clingfilm and chill for at least 1 hour.

Preheat the oven to 175°C.

Prepare four 10cm fluted flan rings on baking sheets or individual flan tins. Divide the pastry into four and roll out each piece to a thickness of about 3mm. Use to line the flan rings, leaving about 15mm overhanging the top to allow for shrinkage. Prick the bases, cover the pastry cases with foil, fill with dried beans and blind bake in the oven for 10–15 minutes. Reduce the oven temperature to 170°C.

For the filling, bring a pan of salted water to the boil. Add the prawns and boil for 2 minutes. Refresh them in a bowl of iced water. Drain the prawns and peel them over a bowl, retaining the shells and any juices. Divide the peeled prawns among the cooked pastry cases.

Place the eggs, milk, cream, chives and seasoning in a bowl and whisk. Taste for seasoning – don't worry, the raw egg won't kill you. Pour enough egg mixture into each flan case to fill it to the top. Bake for 20–25 minutes. The filling should be golden on top and a little wobbly in the centre.

To prepare the prawn and lemon mayonnaise, fry the shallot in a little olive oil in a saucepan. Do not allow the shallot to brown. Add the reserved prawn shells and juice, the bay leaf and parsley stalks. Cook for a minute or so, using a wooden spoon to pound the prawn shells and extract as much flavour as possible from them. Add the wine, bring to the boil, cover and cook for a further minute. Remove the lid and boil the liquid to reduce it, pounding all the time with the wooden spoon. Continue boiling until only 1 tbsp of liquid remains. Strain the cooking liquor into a clean bowl using a very fine Chinoise or a sieve with muslin. Allow the liquid to cool a little before adding the mayonnaise and lemon juice.

Place each warm tart in the middle of a plate. Scatter over some soft herbs and drizzle a little of the mayonnaise onto each plate.

Variations

Wild mushroom and thyme
Lightly sauté 2 handfuls of mushrooms in butter. Add the leaves from 4 sprigs of thyme. Divide between the pastry cases and continue as in the main recipe. Serve with plain mayonnaise.

Lobster and dill
Mix 100g cooked diced lobster meat and 4 sprigs of dill, and divide between the pastry cases. Continue as in the main recipe and serve with plain mayonnaise.

Cashel Blue Tart

Cashel Blue has long since been one of my favourite cheeses and, despite being made in quite large volumes nowadays, it still retains that lovely balance of creamy and sharp flavours. I adore anything prepared using this Irish treasure, including this lovely tart.

Pastry

150g plain flour, plus extra for dusting

75g unsalted butter, cubed

25g Parmesan cheese, grated

1–2 tbsp ice-cold water

1 egg yolk

Filling

2 tbsp polenta

6 spring onions, finely sliced

200g Cashel Blue cheese, crumbled

freshly ground black pepper

3 thyme sprigs

2 egg yolks

3 eggs

400ml double cream

dressed salad leaves and toasted walnuts to serve

SERVES 4–6

To make the pastry, sift the flour into a bowl. Add the butter and Parmesan cheese and rub them into the flour using your fingertips. When the mixture resembles fine breadcrumbs, add the water and egg yolk, and mix thoroughly. Roll the pastry into a ball, wrap it in clingfilm and chill for 30 minutes.

Preheat the oven to 180°C.

On a lightly floured surface, roll out the pastry, giving it a quarter-turn (90°) occasionally, until it is large enough to line a round 20cm wide, 3cm deep, loose-bottomed flan tin. Line the tin with the pastry. The pastry is soft and tricky to roll, but you can patch up any holes or gaps with trimmings and leftovers. Prick the base, cover the pastry case with foil, or greaseproof or parchment paper, fill with dried beans and blind bake for 20 minutes. Remove the beans and foil or paper, and return the case to the oven. Bake for a further 5 minutes to lightly brown and crisp the pastry.

Sprinkle the polenta over the bottom of the baked pastry case, followed by the spring onions and Cashel Blue. Season with black pepper but don't add salt as the cheese is naturally salty. Remove the leaves from the thyme and scatter them over the tart. In a bowl, whisk together the egg yolks, whole eggs and cream and pour this gently into the pastry case.

Slide the tart gently into the oven and bake for 45–60 minutes. Cover it loosely with foil for the last 10–15 minutes if the top is browning too much. The filling should be set, but with a slight wobble.

Serve warm with dressed salad leaves and a few toasted walnuts.

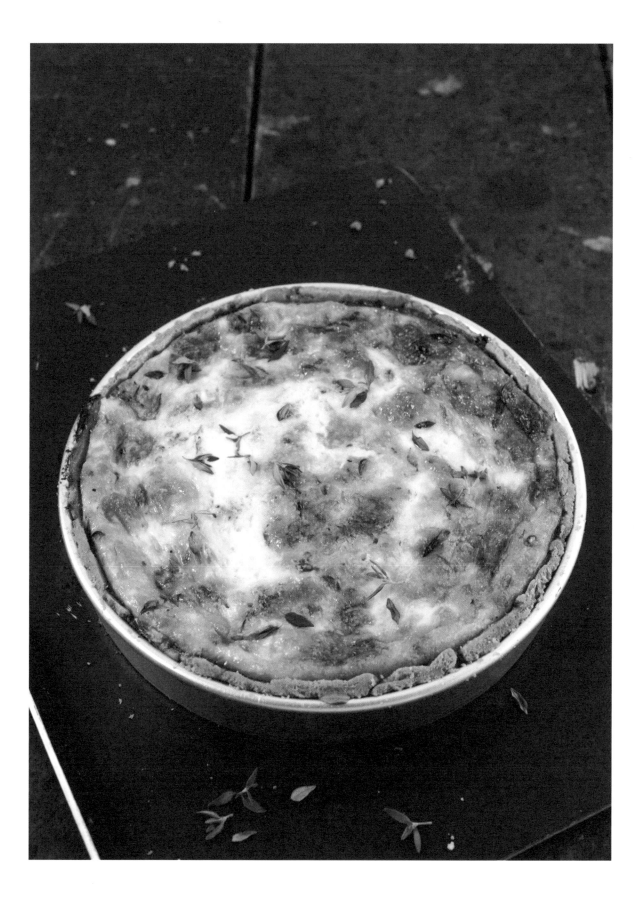

Soup

Soup has long been a favourite first course or light lunch at The Yellow Door. We serve gallons of the stuff, especially in winter, with a selection of our breads, thickly sliced. As with all food, no matter how complex or simple the method, only the best quality ingredients can ensure a perfect result.

Along with the fresh ingredients, the most important element is the stock or liquid used in the soup. As one of my favourite patrons at the deli tells me, 'There's always something better than water'. This colourful lady also offers tips on some other life essentials: 'Drink in a pub, eat in a restaurant and sleep in a hotel'. Good advice.

I have included a few of my favourite soups in this chapter. You will notice the quantities are for a generous eight portions. Make soup in a big pot and, if you don't eat it all on the first day, it will taste even better on the second.

Mushroom Soup with Porcini and Herbs

This soup is incredibly earthy and bursting with rich mushroom flavour. For a posh dinner party, add a dollop of crème fraîche, some chopped chives and a drizzle of truffle oil to each bowl before serving.

4 tbsp olive oil

1.5kg large flat-cap mushrooms, roughly chopped

2 onions, roughly chopped

4 garlic cloves, roughly chopped

2 celery sticks, roughly chopped

½ leek (white part only), roughly chopped

1.5 litres chicken, beef or vegetable stock

2 bay leaves

2 sprigs each of parsley, rosemary, thyme and sage, tied tightly together with string

100g dried porcini

100ml cream (optional)

salt and freshly ground black pepper

bunch of flat-leaf parsley, chopped

SERVES 8–10

I suggest using two large pans initially as this will speed the cooking process up. Heat both pans on a high heat and add 2 tablespoons of olive oil to each one. Divide the mushrooms between the pans and cook, stirring regularly. The secret of this soup is not to overcrowd the pan and to cook the mushrooms for quite a long time. You want the mushrooms to cook gently, not boil.

After about 10 minutes, when the mushrooms have reduced considerably in bulk, add the onions, garlic, celery and leek. Cook for a further 5 minutes. Transfer all the vegetables to one pot, add the stock, bay leaves and bunch of herbs, and bring to the boil. Turn the heat down so that the soup simmers gently.

Place the porcini in a small bowl and pour in about 100ml boiling water. Leave to soak for 5–10 minutes. Take the porcini from the water and add them to the soup. Strain the porcini soaking liquid through muslin or a very fine tea strainer into the soup.

Simmer the soup for 45 minutes. Remove the bunch of herbs and bay leaves. Blend the soup in a blender until smooth. The soup will be very dark in colour – if you prefer to lighten the colour and enrich the soup, add 100ml of cream. Season to taste and reheat if necessary. Sprinkle with the chopped parsley just before serving.

Rich Tomato and Parmesan Soup

The whole art of making soup is to mix appropriate flavours, skilfully eking as much flavour as possible out of the ingredients to deliver a sublime bowl of soup. I hate wasting any ingredient that has culinary merit. In this recipe I use the Parmesan crust that is left after the softer centre has been grated away. The crust of the cheese softens while cooking and imparts a rich, creamy, slightly salty flavour that lifts this tomato soup to another level.

olive oil for cooking

2 onions, roughly chopped

2 celery sticks, roughly chopped

4 garlic cloves, roughly chopped

1 glass dry white wine

500ml chicken or vegetable stock

2 bay leaves

2 sprigs each of parsley, rosemary, thyme and sage, tied tightly together with string

4 x 400g cans chopped tomatoes

½ tsp brown sugar

150–175g Parmesan cheese rind, or 75g Parmesan cheese, finely grated

large bunch of basil

juice of ½ lemon

salt and freshly ground black pepper

SERVES 8–10

Heat around 4 tablespoons of oil in a large pan over medium heat. Add the onions, celery and garlic and fry, stirring, for 2–3 minutes until softened but not browned. Add the wine, stock, bay leaves, tied herbs and chopped tomatoes.

Bring the soup to the boil and then reduce the heat so that it simmers gently. Add the sugar and Parmesan rind (if using grated Parmesan do not add at this stage). Cover and simmer gently for 1 hour.

Remove the bay leaves, tied herbs and Parmesan rind from the pan and purée the soup in a blender until smooth. Remove the leaves from the basil and tear them into pieces. Add the basil to the soup with the lemon juice and grated Parmesan (if using). Blend for a further 30 seconds.

Season the soup to taste and serve it hot, with plain ciabatta bread.

Vichyssoise

Vichyssoise sounds very exotic but, in fact, it's nothing more than a cold leek and potato soup, and is just as delicious and easy to make. Try this really well chilled – I promise you'll enjoy it.

olive oil for cooking

50g butter

6–8 leeks (white part only), finely sliced

2 shallots, finely diced

1 garlic clove, finely chopped

1 glass white wine

1 litre chicken stock

3 medium floury potatoes, cut into 1cm dice

2 bay leaves

350ml double cream

1 bunch of chives

1 bunch of flat-leaf parsley

salt and freshly ground black pepper

pinch of freshly grated nutmeg

SERVES 8–10

Heat a little olive oil with the butter in a large pan over medium heat. When the butter has melted and is hot, add the leeks, shallots and garlic, and cook for 3–5 minutes, or until soft.

Pour in the wine and bring to the boil, then add the chicken stock, potatoes and bay leaves. Bring to the boil, reduce the heat so that the soup simmers and cover the pan. Simmer for 25–30 minutes.

Add the cream, chives and parsley and allow to cook for another minute. Remove from the heat, take out the bay leaves and purée the soup in a blender until smooth. Season with salt, pepper and nutmeg. Strain the soup through a fine sieve, allow to cool and then chill thoroughly before serving. I usually place the bowls in which I'm going to serve the soup in the freezer one hour before serving to ensure that they are really cold.

Roasted Spiced Butternut Squash Soup

A chilli-spiked winter's day wonder. Don't throw away the seeds from the squashes – toss them a little olive oil, season generously and roast in a hot oven for 10–15 minutes. They make a delicious snack.

2–3 butternut squash,
total weight about 3.5–4kg

3 tbsp olive oil

salt and freshly ground black pepper

2 onions, chopped

2 celery sticks, chopped

2 garlic cloves, chopped

½ tsp ground cumin

¼ tsp cayenne pepper

¼ tsp ground coriander

¼ tsp ground ginger

¼ tsp dried chilli flakes

3 star anise

2 litres chicken or vegetable stock

150ml double cream or coconut milk

crème fraîche, to garnish

handful of coriander, chopped, to garnish

SERVES 8–10

Preheat the oven to 190°C.

Cut the squashes in half, remove their seeds and place them, cut-side up, in a roasting tin. Brush each half with olive oil, using a total of 2 tablespoons. Season with salt and pepper, and roast for 45–60 minutes until the flesh is soft.

Meanwhile, heat the remaining olive oil in a large pan. Fry the onions, celery and garlic for about 5 minutes, stirring, but do not allow them to colour. Add the cumin, cayenne pepper, ground coriander, ginger, chilli flakes and star anise and continue cooking for a further 3 minutes. Pour in the stock and bring to a gentle simmer.

Remove and discard the squash skins, and roughly chop the flesh. Add the squash to the soup and simmer for a further 20 minutes.

Remove the star anise and purée the soup with a stick blender, or in batches in a blender, until smooth. Add the cream or coconut milk and season to taste. Reheat gently, if necessary, without boiling.

Ladle into warmed bowls and top each one with a dollop of crème fraîche and chopped coriander.

Leek, Potato and Bacon Soup

This hearty soup is best served with crusty bread and lots of good Irish butter.

1 tbsp olive oil

4 dry-cure bacon rashers, diced

2 onions, diced

4 celery sticks, diced

1 garlic clove, chopped

1.5 litre chicken or ham stock

1 bay leaf

1 sprig each of parsley, rosemary and thyme, tied together with string

4 potatoes, diced

1 large leek, thinly sliced

splash of double cream

salt and freshly ground black pepper

SERVES 8–10

Heat the olive oil in a large pan over a medium heat. Add the bacon and fry, stirring, until it starts to colour. Add the onions, celery and garlic and continue cooking over medium heat for 3–4 minutes. Don't let the vegetables brown.

Add the stock, bay leaf and tied herbs, and bring to the boil. Add the potatoes and simmer over low heat for 20–25 minutes. Add the leek and simmer for a further 5 minutes. Remove the herbs, add the cream and season to taste. Serve immediately.

Variations

Leek, Potato and Smoked Haddock Soup
Add 350g undyed smoked haddock, skinned and cut into 3cm chunks, with the leeks. Use 2 litres of fish stock instead of the chicken stock. The bacon works really well with the smoky fish, but you can leave it out if you want a meat-free soup.

Leek, Potato and Chicken Soup
Add 2 skinless boneless free-range chicken breasts, diced into 2.5cm pieces, with the potatoes. You may also need to add extra stock as the chicken makes the soup more chunky.

Barbecued Langoustines with Lime, Coriander and Smoked Chilli

Provide fingerbowls for your guests when you serve these delicious langoustines. You can buy dried smoked chillies in good delis (like The Yellow Door!), but if you can't find them, dried chilli flakes make a good substitute.

1 garlic clove, very finely chopped

1 tsp finely chopped dried smoked chilli, or dried chilli flakes

grated zest and juice of 2 limes

bunch of coriander leaves, chopped, plus extra to garnish

5 tbsp olive oil

salt and freshly ground black pepper

16–20 langoustines, halved lengthways

2 limes, cut into wedges, to serve

SERVES 4

Either light a charcoal barbecue or preheat a grill on high.

Make the dressing by mixing the garlic, chilli, lime zest and juice, coriander and olive oil. Add seasoning to taste.

Lay out the langoustines, cut-side up, on a dish and brush them liberally with the dressing. Season with salt and pepper. Barbecue or chargrill the langoustines over high heat for 1–2 minutes on each side.

Divide the langoustines among four long plates, spoon any remaining dressing over them and finish with some fresh coriander springs and wedges of lime. Serve immediately.

Smoked Chicken Fillet

The end result of this process should be smoky, succulent chicken – great with salads, as a warm first course or in a sandwich. It's easy to smoke food at home either using a hot pan and some wood chips or a Bradley Smoker. The method works equally well for fish and meat, so do some experimenting.

1 litre water

300g rock salt

3 tarragon sprigs

3 marjoram sprigs

grated zest of ½ lemon

1 bay leaf

1 tsp black peppercorns

8 boneless chicken breasts, skin on

smoke chips

4 thyme sprigs

SERVES 8

Place the water, salt, tarragon, marjoram, lemon zest, bay leaf and peppercorns in a saucepan. Bring to the boil, stirring all the time to dissolve the salt. When the salt has dissolved, remove the pan from the heat and set the brine aside until completely cool.

Prick the chicken skin all over with a skewer. Place the chicken breasts in the cold brine and leave to cure for 6 hours. At this point the chicken can be drained, thoroughly dried with a clean tea towel and smoked immediately or placed in the fridge.

Use one of the two hot smoking methods below to cook the chicken, and showcase your culinary ingenuity. Alternatively, try method three and buy your smoked products from an expert smoker.

Method One: Oven method
This easy and fast hot smoking method is suitable only for small, flat food items, such as salmon and other similar fish portions or small pieces of chicken (for example boneless breast fillets), pheasant, duck or venison. It is important to ensure that you have everything ready before you add the chips to the hot pan because the wood chips begin to smoke a lot very quickly.

You need an ovenproof pan or baking tin with a tight-fitting lid. The pan must be large enough to hold the chicken (or food to be smoked) in a single layer and deep enough to contain the wood chips, plus a layer of foil on which to place the food. An ovenproof skillet (deep lidded frying pan) or covered roaster is ideal. If the lid does not fit tightly, prepare a band of foil to scrunch around the outside edge of the lid and over the lip of the pan to seal in the smoke.

You'll need a good handful of wood chips (widely available online) and you can also add robust herbs, such as rosemary, thyme, bay or sage, at the same time as the chips.

Preheat the oven to 150°C.

To make a platform for the chicken fillets to sit on during smoking, lightly oil a piece of foil and scrunch it up until it is slightly smaller than the pan. The foil should raise the chicken around 2.5cm above the bottom of the pan, to prevent the chicken from scorching and allow it to smoke and cook evenly. Lay the chicken fillets on the foil.

Heat the pan over medium heat. When it is hot, add the wood chips, quickly place the chicken on foil on top and cover immediately with a lid. Scrunch foil over the edge of the lid and pan, if necessary, to prevent smoke from escaping.

Cook in the oven for 5–6 minutes. To check that the chicken is cooked use a thermometer, which should register a temperature of at least 75°C. If the chicken needs a little longer, replace the lid and leave in the smoker for a few more minutes.

Method Two: The Bradley Smoker
Follow the manufacturer's instructions for using the appliance. As a guide, use applewood, maple or cherry chips for poultry or game; and oak, beech or mesquite for fish. Place the chicken on the trays in the Bradley Smoker. Set the heat setting to ⅔ heat and smoke the chicken for 1 hour. Fish takes 30–45 minutes.

Method Three: Buy from the experts
Frank Hederman
Walter Ewing
Woodcock Smokery
Gubbeen Smoke House
Ummera Smoke House

Smoked Eel and Pancetta Salad

I know that some of you may not have a vast lough, like Lough Neagh, on your doorstep, so obtaining eels may be a little problematic. If you can find it, smoked eel is well worth the trouble, or freshly smoked mackerel or herrings make a very good alternative.

100g pancetta or streaky bacon, thinly sliced

300g smoked Lough Neagh eel, skinned, filleted and cut into 3cm pieces

salt and freshly ground black pepper

½ bulb of fennel, very thinly sliced

3 good handfuls of mixed baby leaf sharp salad leaves, such as frisée or chicory

1 tbsp olive oil

squeeze of lemon juice

20 cherry vine tomatoes, halved

Crème fraîche dressing

2 tbsp crème fraîche

juice of 1 lemon

1 tsp finely grated fresh horseradish

2 tsp chopped dill

SERVES 4

Preheat the grill on high. Lay the pancetta or bacon in a grill pan or tray and cook under the grill until crisp. Turn off the grill and add the eel to the pan to warm slightly. Leave under the grill until the salad is ready.

For the crème fraîche dressing, mix the crème fraîche with the lemon juice, horseradish, dill and seasoning, and set aside. Place the fennel and salad leaves in a bowl. Dress lightly with the olive oil, a squeeze of lemon juice and seasoning.

Divide the dressed salad among four plates. Add the pancetta, eel and cherry tomatoes. Drizzle a little of the crème fraîche dressing over the top and serve immediately.

Gravad Lax of Salmon

I do hope that you try this recipe, which is not at all difficult and very rewarding to make. You just have to use good salmon and take a little time. Gravad lax freezes well but when I make it I'm always nipping little pieces off to eat, so there is never enough to get to the freezer.

700g rock salt

225g light Demerara sugar

1 tbsp freshly ground black pepper

1 salmon, weighing approximately 3.6 kg, cleaned, filleted and pinboned (ask your fishmonger to do this)

large bunch of dill, roughly chopped

10 tbsp Pernod or vodka if you prefer something milder

SERVES 30

Begin making the gravad lax 3–4 days in advance. Mix the salt, sugar and pepper together in a bowl. Place three layers of clingfilm, the length of the salmon plus 10cm at each end, on top of one another on a board. Sprinkle 3 tablespoons of the salt mixture towards the centre of the clingfilm and place both fillets on the clingfilm, skin-side down. Divide the rest of the salt mixture between the flesh sides of the fillets and sprinkle the Pernod or vodka over them. Using the clingfilm to help, flip one fillet on top of the other and wrap in clingfilm, enclosing the fish completely. The two fillets should be back in the shape of a whole fish. Tie up the ends, place the salmon in a shallow dish, place a tray on top of the fish and weigh it down with cans or similar weights. Leave in the fridge for 3 days. Turn the fish over every 12 hours, taking care to ensure that the curing mix does not fall out from between the fillets.

Wash the curing mix from the salmon under running cold water and dry the fillets thoroughly with a clean tea towel. Sprinkle the dill over the flesh side of each fillet. Wrap each side tightly in clingfilm and chill. The gravad lax is now ready to eat. It will keep in the fridge for about a week or it can be frozen for 2–3 months.

To serve, slice the gravad lax with a sharp knife very thinly at a 45° angle.

Horseradish Panna Cotta

The gravad lax (opposite) makes a really sophisticated first course when served with horseradish panna cotta.

2 gelatine leaves

550ml single cream

1 strip of lemon zest

1 tbsp Irish whiskey

good pinch of salt

100g good quality creamed horseradish

4 twists of freshly ground black pepper, plus extra to serve

SERVES 6

Place the gelatine leaves in a bowl and pour in cold water to cover. Leave to soak for 15 minutes until softened. Mix the cream, lemon zest, whiskey, salt, horseradish and pepper in a saucepan. Bring to the boil, stirring all the time to dissolve the salt. Remove from the heat and take out the lemon zest.

Take the gelatine leaves out of the cold water and squeeze off any excess moisture. Add the gelatine to the hot cream and stir until it is completely dissolved. Strain the mixture into a jug, and then divide among six ramekins. Allow to cool. Then cover the dishes with clingfilm and place in the fridge to set for at least 2 hours.

To serve, dip each ramekin dish into boiling water and turn them out into the centres of individual plates. Surround them with strips of gravad lax, some baby herbs and a drizzle of olive oil, and grind some black pepper over the top.

Irish Whiskey-marinated Smoked Salmon

500g sea salt

150g unrefined brown sugar

2 tbsp roughly chopped thyme leaves

1 salmon, weighing approximately 3.6 kg, cleaned, filleted and pinboned (ask your fishmonger to do this)

2½ tbsp Irish whiskey

SERVES 30

Mix the salt, sugar and thyme in a bowl. Place three layers of clingfilm, the length of the salmon plus 10cm at each end, on top of one another on a board. Sprinkle 3 tablespoons of the salt mixture towards the centre of the clingfilm and place both fillets on the clingfilm, skin-side down. Divide the rest of the salt mixture between the flesh side of the fillets and sprinkle the whiskey over them. Using the clingfilm to help, flip one fillet on top of the other and wrap in clingfilm, enclosing the fish completely. The two fillets should be back in the shape of a whole fish. Tie up the ends, place the salmon in a large shallow dish, place a tray on top and weigh it down with cans or similar weights. Place in the fridge for 4–6 hours or overnight, turning once. Rinse off the salt in cold water and dry the salmon thoroughly with a clean tea towel.

Cut the salmon into portions for hot smoking and use one of the methods given in the Smoked Chicken Fillet recipe (pages 66–7). Alternatively follow the manufacturer's instructions and use a cold smoker. As a guide, the sides of salmon will probably need 5–8 hours in a cold smoker. Turn the smoker off and allow the salmon to rest before use.

A hot-smoked salmon portion will keep for 3–4 days. Cold-smoked salmon, tightly wrapped, will keep for 1–2 weeks.

Soused Lough Neagh Pollen

Pollen is not a very well known species of fish in Ireland, despite there being fairly large numbers of them in Lough Neagh. They are a type of freshwater herring, about the size of a sardine, with beautiful silver skin. Use herring or small mackerel in this recipe if you can't find pollen. Pollen's oily flesh can be cooked in the same way as mackerel, and they make a really tasty addition to a summer picnic or barbecue. I've included this recipe not only because I like pollen this way, but also because I usually receive them by the bucketful, and sousing is an effective way of dealing with at least half a bucket.

20 pollen, scaled, filleted and boned

350ml white wine vinegar

½ glass of dry white wine

1 shallot, finely sliced

1 fennel bulb, finely sliced

10 cloves

1 dsp rock salt

1 tsp black or green peppercorns

2 tsp sugar

4 bay leaves

SERVES 20

Preheat the oven to 140°C.

Roll up the pollen fillets, skin side facing out, and secure each one by skewering with a cocktail stick. Place the fillets in a heavy roasting tin or cast iron casserole, ensuring that they fit snugly.

Pour the white wine vinegar and white wine into a saucepan and bring to the boil over medium heat. Sprinkle the shallot, fennel, cloves, salt, peppercorns and sugar over the fillets. Pour the boiling vinegar and wine over the top and add the bay leaves. Cover with a lid or a double layer of foil and place in the oven for 30–40 minutes.

Remove the fish from the oven. Take one fillet from the centre of the pot and squeeze it between your finger and thumb. If the fish feels firm – not jelly-like – it's ready. Then replace the lid and allow the fish to cool in the cooking liquor.

Once cooled, the pollen are ready to eat; however, they will keep in their cooking liquor for up to 10 days in the fridge. Serve with shaved fennel, salad leaves and Aïoli (page 34).

Little Gem, Pear and Bellingham Blue Salad with Toasted Walnuts

Bellingham Blue makes a dressing that is deliciously creamy and full-flavoured. It is perfect for firm lettuce leaves, like Cos, Little Gem and endive, and is particularly good with pears.

100g walnuts

4–6 Little Gem lettuces

2 firm pears (such as Beurre Hardy or Conference)

Bellingham Blue dressing

3 tbsp Mayonnaise (page 34)

2 tbsp crème fraîche

1 tsp Dijon mustard

1 tsp extra-virgin olive oil

juice of ½ lemon

150g Bellingham Blue, or similar sharp blue cheese, crumbled

salt and freshly ground black pepper

SERVES 4–6

First make the dressing. Purée the mayonnaise, creme fraîche, mustard, olive oil, lemon juice and half the cheese in blender. Pour the dressing into a bowl, stir in the remaining cheese and check the seasoning. This method ensures that you have a creamy dressing with a good blue cheese flavour and some extra pieces of cheese in the dressing.

Heat a frying pan over medium heat without adding any oil. Add the walnuts and toast them, shaking the pan and turning them, until they are lightly browned. Watch them carefully as they burn easily.

Quarter the Little Gems and divide them among four serving bowls. Quarter and core the pears, and then slice them thinly. Scatter the pear slices in the bowls.

Spoon several tablespoons of dressing over the lettuce and pears. (The remaining dressing will keep well in the fridge for up to 7 days.) Scatter the walnuts over the top, crushing the odd walnut as you go. Serve immediately.

Jilly's Goat's Cheese, Beetroot and Toasted Pine Nut Salad

One of my wife's recipes, this salad is a favourite of mine.

10 young beetroot

2 tbsp balsamic vinegar

2 tbsp olive oil, plus extra for drizzling

salt and freshly ground black pepper

30g pine nuts

5 celery sticks, thinly sliced

100g Ryefield, St Tola or other good goat's cheese

handful of flat-leaf parsley, chopped

SERVES 6

Preheat the oven to 180°C.

Wash the beetroots and trim off their leaves, leaving about 3cm of stalk and root at each end. Do not peel. Wrap them in foil and bake for 45–60 minutes. Test the beetroot with a skewer or fork to check if they are cooked: they should be tender but still have some firmness. Remove from the oven and leave to rest for 5 minutes.

Peel the beetroots while hot by rubbing off the skin, which should come away easily, and cut them into wedges about 2cm thick. Place the wedges in a bowl and sprinkle over the balsamic vinegar, olive oil and a little salt and pepper.

Stir to coat the beetroot thoroughly with the dressing. Allow to cool for 15–20 minutes.

Heat a frying pan over medium heat without adding any oil. Add the pine nuts and toast them, shaking the pan and turning them frequently, until golden. Watch the pine nuts closely as they burn easily.

Add the pine nuts and celery to the beetroot and mix well. Transfer the salad to the serving plate and crumble the goat's cheese over the top. Finally, sprinkle with parsley and add a quick drizzle of olive oil before serving.

Paul's Game Terrine

This recipe uses duck leg meat but you can use pigeon, pheasant, rabbit, venison or any game, in any combination – opportunism is the name of the game – as long as you add the belly of pork. Game tends to be lean, so the extra pork fat is vital. A friend once gave me sixty pigeons after he'd spent a particularly productive day clearing his land. By 11 o'clock that night I was glad to see the last breast fillet go into the freezer. It always seems to be feast or famine with game, so it is useful to have a few recipes up your sleeve, like this tasty terrine. In France, they often use pig's caul to line the mould instead of bacon. The white webbing looks beautiful and transforms this dish into something more elegant, but it's not easy to find. Serve the terrine cut thick on crusty bread with some cornichons or dill gherkins on the side and a glass of sloe gin. It's best made a day or so in advance and will keep in the fridge for two or three days.

500g dry-cure streaky bacon rashers

400g boneless, skinless duck leg meat

400g pork belly, cubed

150g chicken livers

25ml Armagnac

25ml Madeira

50ml dry white wine

50g dried cranberries

2 tsp chopped thyme

salt and freshly ground black pepper

1 x 250g jar foie gras, chilled and sliced (optional)

SERVES 6–8 (A COUPLE OF SLICES EACH)

Preheat the oven to 180°C.

Stretch the bacon rashers with the back of a knife to lengthen them, then use to line a 1.2 litre terrine, measuring about 25 x 8cm, and 6cm deep. The rashers should be long enough to line the terrine with some overhang.

Blitz the duck, pork and chicken livers in a food processor for a couple of seconds, using the pulse button. Don't overprocess the mixture, as it should be chunky. Scrape the meat into a bowl and add the Armagnac, Madeira, wine, cranberries and thyme. Season well and mix thoroughly.

Spoon the mixture into the terrine, smooth it down and fold the overhanging bacon over the top. If using the foie gras, spoon half the mixture in, add a layer of foie gras, then spoon over the remaining duck mixture. Cover tightly with a lid or foil.

Place the terrine in a roasting tin and pour in hot water to half-fill the roasting tin. Bake for 1½ hours. Don't worry if your terrine shrinks and gives out quite a lot of liquid during cooking. Leave the terrine to cool slightly, then remove the lid and cover with a double layer of clingfilm and double-thick foil. Weight the terrine lightly and cool completely, then chill. Turn out before serving.

Chicken Liver Pâté

This very easy recipe makes a deliciously smooth pâté. It's really great with sourdough bread or baguette, as a first course or as part of a summer picnic.

500g chicken livers

150g butter

1 garlic clove, finely chopped

1 good measure of brandy or Bushmill's whiskey

100ml double cream

salt and freshly ground black pepper

SERVES 10

Wash the livers really well and trim off any green or discoloured bits. Heat a deep sauté pan over medium heat. Add half the butter and when it froths add the chicken livers in one layer, without crowding the pan too much. You may have to cook the livers in two batches. They should be lightly golden all over. When they're all ready, return the first batch to the pan, if necessary, and add the garlic. Cook for 20–30 seconds, shaking the pan all the time.

Add the whiskey or brandy and stand well back in case it flames. You don't have to flame the whiskey but it will probably catch anyway if you are cooking on gas. Cook for a further 30 seconds.

Empty the contents of the pan into a food processor. Add the rest of the butter and the cream, and process until you have a smooth, soft pâté. Taste to check the seasoning.

Pass the mixture through a fine sieve. Then spoon it into a terrine or bowl and leave to cool. When it is cold you might like to pour a little melted clarified butter on top. Cover with clingfilm and chill. It will keep well for 5–6 days.

Pan-seared Woodpigeon with Puy Lentils, Lamb's Lettuce and Roasted Walnut Dressing

Having been brought up in the countryside, with a father who is a keen huntsman, I have been taught to appreciate and respect wild animals. I would rather eat pigeon or another game bird that has had a good life, living wild and eating natural food, than some unfortunate battery chicken that was unable to function normally in an overcrowded growing facility. So I would encourage everyone to give game a chance.

200g Puy lentils

salt and freshly ground black pepper

4 woodpigeon breast fillets

leaves from 1 thyme sprig, chopped

olive oil for cooking

25g butter

small bunch of lamb's lettuce

Dressing

25g walnuts, roughly chopped

4 tbsp extra-virgin olive oil

½ tbsp walnut oil

½ tbsp Jerez sherry vinegar or balsamic vinegar

SERVES 4

Place the lentils in a saucepan and pour in 750ml water. Do not add salt at this stage (it will make the lentils tough). Bring to the boil, reduce the heat and cover the pan, then simmer the lentils for 15–18 minutes. Drain and return the lentils to the pan. Cover to retain the heat and set aside.

Meanwhile, make the dressing. Heat a frying pan over medium heat, without adding oil. Add the walnuts and toast them until they are golden. Watch the nuts carefully as they burn easily. Allow to cool and then roughly chop the nuts. Place in a bowl and mix in the olive and walnut oils, and vinegar. Season to taste. Mix the lentils with two-thirds of this dressing and set aside.

Season the fillets thoroughly on both sides and sprinkle with thyme. Heat a sauté pan over medium-high heat. Add a splash of olive oil and sear the fillets on both sides. Add the butter and cook the fillets for 3–4 minutes, basting occasionally. They should be medium-rare. Remove from the pan and allow to rest for 5 minutes.

Divide the lentils among the centres of four warmed plates and arrange the lamb's lettuce around them. Slice each pigeon fillet into three at a 45 degree angle and arrange on top of the lentils. Spoon the remaining dressing over the top and around the plate, and serve immediately.

Pan-seared Foie Gras with Caramelised Apples and Roasted Hazelnut Dressing

This is probably one of the richest first courses I cook. It is reserved for very special occasions because, firstly, it's expensive to make and, secondly, because it is truly decadent and really rockets your cholesterol count. I think once in a while, what the hell.

olive oil for cooking

3 Cox's Orange Pippin apples, cored and cut into thin wedges (about 10 per apple)

2 knobs of butter

1 tbsp unrefined brown sugar

salt and freshly ground black pepper

6 slices of brioche

1 frisée lettuce, all outer leaves remove and white centre finely picked into small sprigs

1 lobe of fresh foie gras, deveined

Dressing

1 tbsp hazelnuts

100ml extra-virgin olive oil

50ml hazelnut oil

1 tbsp aged balsamic vinegar

½ tbsp finely chopped chives

squeeze of lemon juice

SERVES 6

Preheat the oven to 140°C. Place six plates in the oven to warm.

To make the dressing, heat a frying pan over medium heat, without adding oil. Add the hazelnuts and toast them until they are golden. Watch them carefully, shaking the pan occasionally, as they burn easily. Cool and roughly chop the nuts, then mix them with the olive and hazelnut oils, the vinegar, chives and lemon juice. Place in a bowl with all the other dressing ingredients. Check the seasoning and set aside.

Place a sauté or frying pan over medium heat. Add a little olive oil and half the apple wedges, ensuring that all the wedges are flat on the hot surface. When one side of each wedge is brown, turn it to brown the other side. Add a knob of butter and sprinkle half the sugar over the apples. Keep shaking the pan so that all the apples are well caramelised. Season lightly with salt. Place the apples on a baking tray and put in the oven to keep warm. Rinse the pan and repeat the process with the remaining oil, apples, butter and sugar. (You may prepare the dish to this point in advance.)

Toast the brioche until the slices are golden brown on each side. Using a 7.5cm round cutter, cut the centre out of each slice and place on the tray alongside the apples. Keep warm in the oven.

Place the apples in a row in the centres of six warm plates. Lay the slices of brioche on top and spoon around a little of the dressing. Place a pinch of the frisée lettuce at the top of each plate.

Slice the foie gras into 12 slices, about 1.2cm thick and season thoroughly on both sides. Heat two sauté pans over high heat. With the extractor fan on full, add the foie gras slices to the hot dry pans. Turn them quickly and then place straight on the brioche – the foie gras should take just 45–60 seconds to cook. There will be some large and some small slices, so arrange them so that each plate has one large and one small slice slightly overlapping on the brioche. Serve immediately.

Carpaccio of Venison with Pickled Walnuts, Parsley Cress and Horseradish Crème Fraîche

If you can't get your hands on venison, use a small piece of beef fillet instead. Parsley cress and other micro-herbs are very popular in restaurants at the moment. They look great and taste nice too, but where do you get them? You could ask your favourite restaurant to order some for you, grow them yourself on a little tray on your window sill or, if you wait a while, your supermarket will be selling them soon, I bet.

10cm piece of venison loin, eye of meat only, trimmed and sinew removed

olive oil

salt

1 tsp Dijon mustard

50g porcini powder or dust (If you cannot buy this product, buy dried porcini or wild mushrooms and grind in a coffee blender or food processor. Sieve to ensure the porcini dust is very fine before use.)

¼ teaspoon freshly ground black pepper

olive oil for cooking

6 pickled walnuts, sliced

50g young parsley seedlings

drizzle of really good extra-virgin olive oil

Horseradish crème fraîche

1 tsp grated fresh horseradish

2 tbsp crème fraîche or sour cream

squeeze of lemon juice

SERVES 4

Brush the venison loin thoroughly with oil and season generously with salt only. Heat a frying pan on a high heat. Seal the venison loin for just a few seconds on each side. Remove from the pan and allow to cool. When the venison is cool, brush all over with the mustard.

Mix the porcini dust and pepper together on a plate. Roll the venison in this mixture until it is evenly coated on all sides. Wrap the venison tightly in clingfilm and chill.

Prepare the horseradish crème fraiche by mixing the horseradish, crème fraîche or sour cream, lemon juice and seasoning in a bowl. Cover and chill.

If you have a friendly butcher, you could now ask him or her to slice your carpaccio into paper-thin slices, using a machine, or you can do it yourself using your sharpest knife. It will be much easier to slice if the venison is really cold – I often freeze it for a couple of hours before slicing.

Present the dish by laying the very thin slices of venison all over four plates. Drizzle the horseradish crème fraiche over the top, and sprinkle the pickled walnuts and parsley seedlings on top. Finally drizzle some of your best olive oil over each plate. Serve immediately.

Pan-seared Slow-cooked Pork Belly with Creamed Savoy Cabbage and Whiskey Honey Glaze

This delicious pork dish must be prepared 24 hours in advance and then finished just before you are going to serve it.

2 onions, sliced into rings

2 red apples, cored and sliced into rings

2 bay leaves

1 garlic clove, halved

2 glasses of cider

½ pork belly, skinned and deboned

olive oil for cooking

salt and freshly ground black pepper

rosemary sprig, leaves chopped

thyme sprig, leaves chopped

sage sprig, leaves chopped

3 measures of Irish whiskey

2 measures of runny honey

Creamed cabbage

½ Savoy cabbage, finely sliced

250ml cream

50g butter

pinch of freshly grated nutmeg

SERVES 8–10

Preheat the oven to 170°C.

Place the onions and apple rings in the centre of a roasting tray. Tuck in the bay leaves and garlic and pour the cider over the top. Lightly score the pork belly on both sides and drizzle with a little olive oil. Season both sides well with salt, pepper, rosemary, thyme and sage. Place the pork on top of the onions and apples and roast for 1½–2 hours until extremely tender. Strain off the fat, and reserve the cooking juices. Allow the pork to cool for 30 minutes before transferring it to a clean roasting tray. Place another roasting tray on top and weigh it down with cans or weights and then chill overnight. This process will squeeze most of the fat out of the pork and ensure that it is flat for the next cooking stage. Strain off and reserve the cooking juices; discard the fat.

Pour the whiskey, honey and reserved cooking juices into a small saucepan over medium heat. Bring to the boil and continue to cook over a high heat until the the mixture has reduced to the consistency of double cream. Allow to cool and then chill overnight.

The next day, cook the cabbage in boiling water for 4–5 minutes. When it's cooked, drain and then return to a low heat for a couple of minutes to dry out. Turn up the heat, add the cream, butter, seasoning and nutmeg and continue to cook until the cream has reduced by two-thirds.

Meanwhile, heat a large frying pan over medium heat. Slice the pork belly into 8–10 slices and fry in a little olive oil until brown and crispy on both sides and thoroughly heated through – 6–8 minutes on each side. Heat the glaze over medium heat. To serve, place a spoonful of cabbage on each plate, lay a slice of pork belly on top and brush the top of the pork belly with the glaze. Serve immediately.

Main Courses

Pan-fried Cod with Morcilla, Sauté Potatoes, Roasted Vine Tomatoes and Coriander Pesto / Seafood Stew with Saffron and Tomatoes / Champ / Seared Salmon with Saffron Mash and Warm Leek Vinaigrette / Italian Fish Pie / Pan-fried Sea Bass with Puy Lentils / Mussels with Lemon and Fennel / Pea and Mint Risotto / Potato Pie / Flageolet Bean Stew / Vichy Carrots / Braised Fennel / Braised Potatoes with Black Pudding / Creamed Celeriac Mash / Roast Chicken / Roast Beef / Roast Pork / Roast Lamb / Confit of Duck / Pan-seared Barbary Duck Fillets with Leafy Greens, Pomegranates and Pomegranate Molasses Dressing / Barbecued Spare Ribs / Roast Pork Belly with Roasties / Lamb Shanks with Prunes / Shepherd's Pie with Root Vegetable Mash / Steak / Béarnaise Sauce

Pan-fried Cod with Morcilla, Sauté Potatoes, Roasted Vine Tomatoes and Coriander Pesto

Morcilla, a crumbly Spanish black pudding that falls apart during cooking, is available in good delis and speciality food shops. It imparts an earthy flavour that works really well with the crisp skin and white succulent flakes of the fish.

500g baby potatoes

salt and freshly ground black pepper

olive oil for cooking

4 x 150g cod, hake or halibut portions, scaled and pinboned, skin on

knob of butter

100g morcilla, skinned and cut into 1cm slices

2 shallots, thinly sliced

1 garlic clove, chopped

juice of ½ lemon

Roasted vine tomatoes

6 vine tomatoes

about 2 tbsp olive oil

about 2 tbsp balsamic vinegar

½ garlic clove, chopped

1 tsp chopped rosemary

Coriander pesto

handful of coriander

150ml extra-virgin olive oil

25g pine nuts, toasted

squeeze of lemon juice

1 tsp Parmesan or Desmond cheese, grated

SERVES 4

Make the pesto first: blitz all the ingredients in a food processor until reduced to a paste. Season and set aside.

Preheat the oven to 165°C.

Halve the tomatoes horizontally and place them, cut-side up, in a single layer in a roasting tin. Drizzle with olive oil and balsamic vinegar, and sprinkle over the garlic and rosemary. Season well and roast for 35 minutes.

Cook the baby potatoes in boiling salted water for 12–15 minutes until tender but still a little firm in the middle. Drain and slice the potatoes, then set them aside.

Place a heavy frying pan over high heat, then add a splash of olive oil. Season the fish portions on both sides and place them in the hot pan, skin-side down. To allow the skin to crisp up, do not touch the fish for at least 3–4 minutes. Add a knob of butter to the pan and baste the fish with the melted butter. Turn the portions of fish, reduce the heat and continue to cook for around 3 more minutes, depending on the thickness of the fish. Remove from the heat and allow the fish to rest in the pan.

Heat a little olive oil in a large sauté pan, or deep frying pan, and fry the morcilla over high heat. When it starts to break up, add the shallots and garlic. Cook until the shallots have softened, then add the sliced potatoes. Continue to sauté, flipping the potatoes constantly – it doesn't matter if they break up a little. When the potatoes are hot and have taken on some of the colour from the morcilla, squeeze the lemon juice over the mixture and remove from the heat.

To assemble, divide the potato mixture among four deep bowls. Lay the tomatoes alongside and the cod, skin side up, on top. Add a drizzle of coriander pesto and you're done.

Seafood Stew with Saffron and Tomatoes

This golden-orange fish stew is one of my favourite suppers to share with friends. It is easy to prepare, very versatile and just hits the spot in late summer – a ray of sunshine in a bowl.

3–4 tbsp olive oil

2 onions, thinly sliced

1 leek, white part only, finely sliced

4 garlic cloves, chopped

2 glasses of white wine

1 x 400g can tomatoes

500ml fish stock

pinch of dried chilli flakes

large pinch of saffron threads

grated zest of ½ lemon or orange

2 bay leaves

bunch of marjoram stalks

bunch of parsley stalks

salt and freshly ground black pepper

1.5kg mixed fish, such as hake, mullet and monkfish, skinned, filleted and cut into chunks

500g raw shellfish, such as mussels, clams and prawns, scrubbed and beards removed from mussels

2 tbsp chopped flat-leaf parsley or coriander leaves

SERVES 6

Heat the oil in a large frying pan or skillet. Add the onions, leek and garlic and cook for 3–4 minutes. Do not allow to colour. Add the wine, tomatoes, stock, chilli flakes, saffron and lemon or orange zest. Tie the bay leaves into a bunch with the marjoram and parsley stalks, then add them to the pan with some salt and pepper. Bring to the boil, reduce the heat to low, and simmer for 25 minutes, after which time the tomatoes will have started to break down. Give the tomatoes a squash with a wooden spoon to help them along.

Add the chunks of fish, firmest fish first, and simmer for 10 minutes. Add the shellfish, discarding any open mussels or clams that do not close when tapped, and cook for a further 4–5 minutes until the prawns are cooked and the mussels and clams have opened. Discard any unopened mussels or clams.

Remove the bunch of herbs and add the chopped parsley or coriander. Serve the stew immediately, with big chunks of crusty bread and a bottle of well-chilled crisp white wine.

Mash Talk

Ireland is the adopted home of the humble spud. Where but in Ireland would people drive twenty or thirty miles to buy a half-hundred weight from their favourite farm? You might have overheard these people discussing balls of flour or Kerr's Pinks and assumed they were old rockers talking about their favourite bands from yesteryear. In fact, buying potatoes is a serious business and I'm glad those farmers and their customers still exist.

I admit I am no expert on potatoes when I look at them in a field or in a potato sack, but I can tell you the differences between them when I get them in a pot.

At The Yellow Door we make our mash – such as the ever-popular champ (still the best) – in a particular way. Like a lot of our recipes, it's not good for the waistline, but it tastes fantastic. You'll need the previously mentioned balls-of-flour varieties of potato for best results.

Champ

This method ensures that the flavour of the scallions permeates the mash. Reducing the cream gives a slightly nutty taste and ensures a great flavour without too much sloppiness.

900g potatoes, peeled and cut into even-sized pieces

240ml double cream

8–10 scallions (spring onions), finely sliced

knob of butter

salt and freshly ground black pepper

SERVES 4

Cook the potatoes by simmering them in salted water until they are tender and cooked through. In the meantime, in a separate large saucepan, boil the cream until it is reduced by two-thirds. Watch the cream carefully as it is likely to boil over or catch on the bottom of the pan. Add the scallions to the cream and remove the pan from the heat.

When the potatoes are cooked, drain them and return them to the pan. Place the pot over a very low heat, without a lid, and leave the potatoes to dry out for around 5 minutes. Pass the potatoes through a sieve or potato ricer. Add the cream mixture to the potatoes, with a good knob of butter, and mix well. Season to taste.

Variations

Basil or Coriander or Rocket Mash
Add a finely chopped bunch of basil, coriander or rocket to to the potatoes at the same time as the cream.

Rosemary Mash
Add the finely chopped leaves from 4–5 rosemary sprigs to the cream instead of the scallions.

Chorizo or Black Pudding Mash
Sauté 2 cooking chorizos or 1 black pudding in olive oil. Chop finely and add to the potatoes at the same time as the cream.

Roast Garlic Mash
Roast a bulb of garlic in the oven at 180°C for 20 minutes. Squeeze out the pulp from the cloves and stir into the potatoes at the same time as the cream.

Saffron Mash
Replace the scallions with a good pinch of saffron threads. This will give the mash a wonderful colour and flavour.

Seared Salmon with Saffron Mash
and Warm Leek Vinaigrette

The one thing you must never do with fish is overcook it, and this is especially true of salmon. In fact, like a steak, it benefits from undercooking, retaining moisture and flavour. This dish works equally well as a first course.

4 x 175g portions salmon fillet, pinboned with skin on

olive oil for cooking

salt and freshly ground black pepper

1 quantity of Saffron Mash (page 89)

Leek vinaigrette

150ml extra-virgin olive oil

1 leek, white part only, finely sliced

½ tbsp balsamic or Jerez sherry vinegar

pinch of brown sugar

grated zest and juice of ½ lemon

bunch of coriander, chopped

SERVES 4

Make the leek vinaigrette by heating half the olive oil in a saucepan over medium-low heat. Add the leek and cook it for 5–6 minutes but don't let it colour. Remove from the heat and add the vinegar, sugar, lemon zest and juice. Cool the vinaigrette by adding the remaining olive oil and, lastly, stir in the coriander. Season to taste and set aside.

Heat a frying pan on high heat. Season the salmon fillets generously on both sides. Add a little olive oil to the pan and then add the salmon portions, skin-side down. Do not be tempted to turn or move the salmon. After 45–60 seconds over high heat reduce the heat to low, still leaving the salmon skin-side down. After about 3 minutes, turn the salmon and cook it on the other side for a further minute or so.

Place a spoonful of lovely, fragrant colourful mash in the centre of each plate. Top the mash with the salmon, skin side up, and spoon some of the leek vinaigrette around the plate.

Italian Fish Pie

This is a grown-up, sophisticated pie and not the conventional mash-covered comfort food. It is perfect for a supper party: something of a labour of love, but well worth the effort.

300ml dry white wine

12 garlic cloves

2 lemons

1.5kg mussels, scrubbed and beards removed

300ml semi-skimmed milk

400g undyed smoked haddock fillet

1kg pollack or brill fillets

2kg waxy salad potatoes

300ml olive oil, plus extra for greasing

salt and freshly ground black pepper

1kg ripe tomatoes

handful of flat-leaf parsley, chopped

3 dried chillies, deseeded and crumbled

250g Pecorino cheese, grated

12 fennel seeds, ground

SERVES 8

Preheat the oven to 200°C.

In a large casserole, heat the wine, 4 cloves of garlic and the lemons. Bring to the boil. Add half the mussels, discarding any open ones, and cover. Simmer for about 5 minutes, giving the pot a shake every minute or so. The mussels should open in this time – discard any unopened ones. Remove the mussels with a slotted spoon from the poaching liquor. Next, remove the mussels from their shells, over a bowl to retain all the cooking juices. When finished, repeat this process with the remaining mussels. Set the mussels aside, strain the cooking liquor through muslin or a fine chinois and set this aside also.

Heat the milk in a large pan and poach the fish for 3–5 minutes. Remove the skin, if necessary, and gently break the fish into bite-sized pieces. Set aside.

Scrub the potatoes and slice them very finely, using a mandolin if you have one. Rinse the potatoes in cold water and dry thoroughly. Place in a bowl with a splash of olive oil and season.

Place a pan filled with boiling water over medium heat. Drop the tomatoes into the boiling water in batches of 4 or 5 for 10–25 seconds, depending on ripeness. Remove and plunge into a bowl of iced water. Peel the tomatoes – the skin should come off easily – quarter them, remove the seeds and cut them into strips.

Mix the parsley, chillies, cheese and ground fennel seeds in a bowl. Crush the remaining garlic cloves with a little salt and add to the bowl.

Grease a large oven dish with a little olive oil. Cover the bottom of the dish with half of the potatoes. Now add half the tomatoes, then sprinkle over a third of the parsley mixture. Add all of the fish and shellfish and another third of the parsley mixture. Pour over half the remaining olive oil and half the reserved mussel liquor. Add the remaining potatoes, followed by the rest of the tomatoes and the final third of the parsley mixture. Lastly, pour over the remaining olive oil and mussel liquor.

Cover the pie with foil and bake for 20 minutes. Remove the foil and cook for a further 40 minutes. Leave to cool for about 5 minutes before serving with a crisp green salad and some warm Ciabatta (pages 30–1).

Pan-fried Sea Bass with Puy Lentils

Easy to prepare and cook, and delicious to eat, this is the perfect dish for a simple supper party. If you would prefer not to use pancetta, add a teaspoon of smoked paprika to the vegetables while they're cooking and it will impart a lovely smoky flavour.

250g puy lentils

2 celery sticks, finely diced

1 small carrot, finely sliced

1 small red onion, finely sliced

2 garlic cloves, finely sliced

olive oil for cooking

200g pancetta or smoked streaky bacon, finely chopped

1 bay leaf

3 thyme sprigs

250ml chicken stock

250ml red wine

salt and freshly ground black pepper

4 sea bass fillets, scaled, skin on

50g butter

bunch of flat-leaf parsley, finely chopped

SERVES 4

Place the lentils in a saucepan and pour in 750ml water to cover. Bring to the boil, reduce the heat and cover the pan, then simmer for 15–18 minutes. Don't add salt at this stage or the lentils will not soften. Use a ladle to remove any scum that surfaces during cooking.

In another pan, sweat the celery, carrot, red onion and garlic in a little olive oil over medium heat. After about 7 minutes, add the pancetta or bacon and cook until browned, which will take about 5 minutes. Set aside.

Drain the lentils and then add them to the vegetables and pancetta. Add the bay leaf, thyme, stock and wine, and boil vigorously for 5 minutes or so, until the liquor is reduced and the alcohol is boiled off. Season with salt and pepper, and keep warm over low heat while you cook the fish.

Season the sea bass fillets on both sides with salt and pepper. Heat the butter and olive oil in a frying pan. When the butter starts to foam, add the fish, skin-side down, and cook for 3–4 minutes, occasionally spooning the butter and olive oil over the flesh side. Turn the fillets over and cook for a further minute.

Remove the thyme sprigs and bay leaves from the lentils and stir in the chopped parsley. Place a generous helping of lentils in the middle of each plate and lay a sea bass fillet on top, skin-side up. Serve immediately.

Mussels with Lemon and Fennel

This mussel dish has a bit more gusto than the lighter traditional moules marinières, and is probably best served in autumn or winter.

olive oil for cooking

1 fennel bulb, cored and thinly sliced

1 small onion, finely chopped

4 garlic cloves, finely chopped

1 tsp cumin seeds, crushed

1 tsp coriander seeds, crushed

1 pinch dried chilli flakes

2.5kg mussels, scrubbed and beards removed

salt and freshly ground black pepper

grated zest and juice of 1 lemon

1 glass of white wine

handful of coriander leaves, chopped

SERVES 4

Heat a little olive oil in your largest pot over high heat. Add the fennel and onion and cook for a couple of minutes, until softened. Add the garlic, cumin seeds, coriander seeds and chilli flakes, and cook for a further minute.

Add the mussels, discarding any open ones, season lightly, and add the lemon zest, juice and wine. Cover and cook for 3–4 minutes, shaking the pot occasionally. The mussels should open during cooking – discard any that remain unopened.

Stir in the coriander, and divide the mussels, with plenty of the delicious juices, among four large bowls. Serve with lots of crusty bread, to mop up the juices, and a large plate to collect the empty shells.

Pea and Mint Risotto

If you have any risotto left over from this delicious dish, try shaping it into little balls, rolling them in seasoned flour, beaten egg and extra-fine breadcrumbs mixed with grated Parmesan cheese and black pepper. Then deep-fry them to make a delicious, easy canapé. The little orbs also freeze well before cooking.

250g frozen peas or petit pois (use fresh peas in season)

bunch of mint, finely chopped

150g butter

salt and freshly ground black pepper

1 litre vegetable or chicken stock

olive oil for cooking

1 onion, finely diced

1 leek, white part only, finely diced

300g Arborio rice

50g Parmesan cheese, grated, plus extra to serve

SERVES 4, OR 6 AS A FIRST COURSE

Cook the peas for 1–2 minutes in boiling, salted water. Drain and refresh them under cold running water. Place two-thirds of the peas, the mint, half of the butter and some salt and pepper in a food processor and blitz the mixture to a purée. Set aside.

Heat the stock to simmering point in a saucepan and keep it hot over low heat. This ensures that heat is not lost during the cooking process by adding cold stock to hot rice.

Heat 25g of the remaining butter and a little olive oil in a heavy-bottomed flameproof casserole. Add the onion and leek and sweat gently until softened, which should take about 5 minutes. Pour in the risotto rice and stir well to coat the grains with the hot butter and oil.

Keeping the heat on low level, add a ladleful of hot stock to the rice – it will bubble and hiss. Stir gently until all the stock has been absorbed before you add the next ladleful. Keep repeating this process for about 15 minutes. At this point, taste the rice to see if it is cooked – the grains should be tender but with a little bite.

Once the rice is cooked through, stir in the pea purée and heat until warm. Finally, add the rest of the butter, the remaining peas and the Parmesan, and stir until the butter and cheese have melted. The risotto should be thick and starchy but not at all solid. If it looks too dry, add a little more stock.

Serve immediately, with some extra grated Parmesan.

Potato Pie

This creamy pie uses all our best local produce and can be adapted to accommodate whatever is in the fridge. Add bacon or ham with half a finely grated apple, or layer asparagus or broad beans with the potatoes. If I fancy a change from the basic recipe, I thinly slice a good strong cheese and an onion and mix them with the potatoes. Serve this hot for lunch or supper, or make it for your next picnic. Served cold, the cheese and onion flavour really develops.

400g good quality puff pastry

flour, for dusting

550g waxy potatoes, finely sliced

2 garlic cloves, finely chopped

2 tbsp finely chopped flat-leaf parsley

salt and freshly ground black pepper

2 egg yolks

1 tbsp milk

100ml double cream

SERVES 6

Preheat the oven to 200°C.

Roll out three-quarters of the pastry on a lightly floured surface and use to line a gratin dish. The dish should be large enough to hold all the potatoes.

Put the sliced potatoes, garlic, parsley and seasoning in a bowl. Mix well and then layer the potatoes in the lined dish. Roll out the remaining pastry. Lightly whisk 1 egg yolk with the milk and use this egg wash to moisten the edges of the pastry rim in the dish. Place the pastry lid on top and carefully seal the edges, using a fork or your fingers. Cut a hole in the top to let the steam escape during cooking. Brush the top with egg wash.

Bake the pie for 50 minutes. Lightly whisk the cream and remaining egg yolk. Remove the pie from the oven and, using a funnel, pour the cream mixture into the hole in the top of the pie. Return the pie to the oven to cook for a further 5 minutes.

Leave to cool slightly before serving with a crisp green salad.

Flageolet Bean Stew

This dish goes brilliantly with Confit of Duck (page 110), pan-fried pork chops or meaty fish, such as cod or monkfish.

250g dried flageolet beans, soaked in cold water overnight, or 400g can flageolet or haricot beans

½ onion, finely sliced

3 garlic cloves, roughly chopped

olive oil for cooking

100g dry-cure smoked streaky bacon or pancetta, diced

2 bay leaves

4 thyme sprigs

1 clove

500ml chicken or vegetable stock

salt and freshly ground black pepper

handful of flat-leaf parsley, finely chopped

extra-virgin olive oil to serve

SERVES 4

If you are using dried beans, drain and rinse them thoroughly after their night-time soak, and set aside.

Sweat the onion and garlic in olive oil in a flameproof casserole over low heat until transparent, but not coloured. Add the bacon or pancetta and cook until it is beginning to brown. Add the bay leaves, thyme, clove, beans and chicken stock. Grind in some black pepper and bring to the boil, skimming off any scum that rises to the surface.

Reduce the heat, cover the pan and simmer gently for 50 minutes. Keep an eye on the fluid level and top up with boiling water, if necessary, to keep the beans covered. If you are using canned beans, reduce the cooking time to 20 minutes.

When cooked, the beans should be melting and tender. Add seasoning to taste and stir in the flat-leaf parsley with a couple of glugs of good quality extra-virgin olive oil.

Vichy Carrots

This is a simple and delicious method of cooking carrots, which brings out their natural sweetness. When cooked they will look glossy and irresistible. The last few moments of this method are very important – do not leave the stove during this time or you will end up with burnt carrots.

8 young carrots, peeled and cut into large pieces

pinch of salt

1 dsp caster sugar

knob of butter

SERVES 4

Place the carrots in a saucepan with the salt, sugar and butter. Pour in enough water to half-cover the carrots (so if your carrots are 8cm deep, pour in water to a depth of 4cm). Cover and bring to the boil. Leave the lid on for a minute or two, and then remove, continuing to boil the carrots until all the water evaporates and the sugar and butter begin to caramelise. Keep shaking the pot to prevent the carrots sticking and burning.

Remove from the heat and check the carrots are cooked – they should be tender but with a little bite. If they are undercooked, add a little more water and continue the process. Serve immediately.

Braised Fennel

4 fennel bulbs

salt and freshly ground black pepper

1 glass of white wine

150ml hot chicken or vegetable stock

1 bay leaf

SERVES 4

Preheat the oven to 170°C.

Cut the fennel in half through the centre, and then into quarters, in the same way you would cut a tomato into wedges. Remove most of the fibrous central root part of the fennel, leaving enough to hold the quarters together. Place the fennel in a small casserole or roasting tin and season lightly.

Pour over the wine and stock, and add the bay leaf. Cover and cook in the oven for 45 minutes to 1 hour, until the fennel is soft in the centre. Serve immediately.

Braised Potatoes with Black Pudding

These delicious potatoes are great with Roast Chicken (page 104), grilled lamb or even with fish, such as hake, halibut, cod or monkfish.

1kg floury potatoes

100g butter

olive oil for cooking

4 onions

1 good quality black pudding, crumbled or cut into small pieces

2 garlic cloves, finely chopped

salt and freshly ground black pepper

1 tbsp chopped thyme

good bunch of flat-leaf parsley, chopped

1.4 litres chicken stock

SERVES 4–6

Preheat the oven to 200°C. Heat the stock to simmering point in a pan over medium heat.

Peel the potatoes and cut them into 3–4mm thick slices. Place in a bowl of cold water.

Melt half the butter with a splash of olive oil in a large frying pan or sauté pan. Add the onions and fry, stirring, until they begin to colour. Add the black pudding and garlic and continue cooking until the onions are golden brown and the black pudding is cooked. Season to taste.

Drain the potatoes and dry thoroughly with a tea towel. Arrange one-third of the potatoes in a small roasting tin or earthenware dish. Season with salt and pepper, then spoon over half of the onion and black pudding mixture. Sprinkle over a third of the thyme and parsley.

Repeat this process and then add the final third of the potatoes. Pour over the hot stock, add the remaining herbs and dot the rest of the butter over the top of the dish. Bake for 50–55 minutes, until the potatoes are cooked through, and the top is golden brown.

Creamed Celeriac Mash

This is real winter comfort food and delicious with roasts and curly kale. Make this mash even more indulgent and smooth by adding extra butter and cream at the end.

1 celeriac, peeled and cut into 5cm dice

600ml milk

1 bay leaf

salt and freshly ground white pepper

10 floury potatoes

275ml double cream

¼ teaspoon grated nutmeg

SERVES 6

Place the celeriac in a saucepan. Pour in the milk and add the bay leaf and a little salt. Bring to the boil, reduce the heat and simmer for about 20 minutes, or until tender. While the celeriac is cooking, boil the potatoes in salted water until tender.

Drain the celeriac through a sieve lined with a clean tea towel. Discard the bay leaf, and press the celeriac with a wooden spoon to remove as much of the milk as possible. Drain the potatoes and place them over a low heat to dry out. Push the potatoes through a potato ricer or sieve and set aside.

Pour the cream into a large pan over high heat and boil until reduced by two-thirds. Watch the cream carefully as it is likely to boil over.

Meanwhile, using a hand-held blender, whizz the celeriac to a smooth purée. Add the potato and celeriac to the reduced cream and mix well. Season with salt, pepper and a little nutmeg. Serve immediately.

Roasts

I really love Sunday lunch, especially when it's a roast. It's a time of the week when you're less rushed and can enjoy both the cooking and the eating. Forgive me for going into such detail, but when you're cooking a glorious piece of meat, it's important to get everything right and treat it with respect. Trust me – your lunch will taste even more special as a result. So, some important things to remember when you cook a roast:

Ensure that you are well informed about the origin, source and breed of your meat before you buy.

Remove the meat from the fridge in good time. It should come up to room temperature before it goes into the oven. Depending on the size of the joint, this can take a 1–2 hours.

A food thermometer is indispensable. The only other way to gauge how well your meat is cooked is to cut a hole in it (not a good idea). As a rough guide – rare: 52–55°C; medium: 55–58°C; medium well: 58–64°C; cooked through: 64–70°C; completely cooked: 75°C plus.

Finally, and very, very importantly, allow your roast to rest, covered loosely with foil to retain some heat, before carving. I usually allow 30 minutes, although anything from 15 minutes up is probably okay.

Roast Chicken

A simple roast chicken is what my mum used to cook for us kids on Sundays. It was simply bunged in the oven as we left for church and then taken out as soon as we got home. I always used to hope that the sermon wouldn't be too long for fear that the lunch would be ruined. When we got back, the house was filled with the delicious smell of roasting chicken and I'd run to the oven and make sure all was well.

A good free-range chicken, simply roasted with a few aromatics, is indeed a noble meal, but it's essential to buy the right bird.

Free-range chickens have a much better life than their commercially reared, intensively farmed counterparts. The fact a bird is free range is more important to me than whether or not it's organic – I am a farmer's son and believe firmly that the priority should be the animals' welfare. Ideally, though, the bird should also be organic – what the animal eats impacts on the flavour of the meat.

75g butter, softened

good handful of mixed herbs, such as parsley, tarragon, thyme, chives and marjoram, chopped

olive oil for cooking

3 carrots, quartered

2 onions, quartered

1.8kg free-range organic chicken

salt and freshly ground black pepper

SERVES 4

Preheat the oven to 210°C.

Beat the butter, herbs and and a good splash of olive oil together. Rub this mixture all over the chicken, then season it generously. Place the carrots and onion in a roasting tin, to form a base or trivet for the chicken to cook on. Then place the chicken on top. Roast the chicken for 15–20 minutes. Reduce the temperature to 180°C and roast the bird for a further 45–50 minutes. Baste the chicken with the herby juices three or four times during cooking.

To check whether the chicken is cooked, either use a meat thermometer, or pierce it with a skewer on the thickest part of the thigh. If the juices run clear, you're there, but if the flesh looks pink from blood or there is any sign of blood in the juices, place the chicken back in the oven for another 5 minutes or so.

Allow the chicken to rest for 20 minutes before carving. I use the cooking juices straight from the pan as gravy.

Roast Beef

The best cut for roasting has to be rib on the bone, from a steer bullock or heifer, from a traditional, slow-maturing breed, matured for a minimum of 28 days. The best breeds are Hereford, Angus, White Park, Galloway, Irish Moiled, Dexter, British White or Highland.

1 x 3–4kg rib of beef on the bone

salt and freshly ground black pepper

olive oil or dripping for cooking

2 onions, quartered

2 carrots, quartered

1 head celery, thickly sliced

Gravy

½ bottle red wine

300ml beef stock

SERVES 12–14

Preheat the oven to 200°C.

Season the beef well on all sides. Heat the roasting tin over high heat, add the olive oil or dripping and brown the beef well on all sides, then remove it from the tin. Take the tin off the heat.

Place the onions, carrots and celery in the base of the roasting tin. Put the meat on top and roast for 30–40 minutes. Reduce the heat to 175°C and continue to roast for around 30 minutes, testing the temperature of the meat regularly with your thermometer until it is cooked as you like it. Remove the beef from the oven, cover it loosely with foil and allow it to rest for 30 minutes.

Meanwhile make a simple gravy. Pour away the excess fat from the roasting tin. Place the roasting tin over medium heat and pour in the red wine. Boil, stirring regularly, until it has reduced by half and then add the stock. Bring to the boil again and reduce again until the gravy is at the consistency you like. Strain the gravy, then pour it into a warm jug or gravy boat.

Carve the meat and serve with Champ (page 89), roasties, your favourite vegetables, the gravy, and mustard or horseradish sauce.

Roast Pork

The choice of pork is all important. I know that most types of rare-breed, free-range pork are likely to be more expensive and somewhat more difficult to find, but I would recommend eating a really tasty, small piece of pork than a large piece of commercial tasteless so-called pork. Buy wisely.

If you can't remember all the different varieties, such as Gloucester Old Spot and Tamworth Saddleback, a good rule of thumb is to go to a good local butcher: if he has gone to the trouble of naming the pig species on his labels, chances are his meat is worth buying. You can use the same philosophy for most meat bought in the butchers or the supermarket.

½ loin of rare-breed pork (weighing approximately 2–2.5kg), skin on

1 small bunch of thyme

salt and freshly ground black pepper

olive oil for cooking

4 sweet red apples, such as Cox's Orange Pippin or Epicure, quartered and cored

½ bottle dry white wine or dry cider

SERVES 10

Preheat the oven to 220°C.

Score the skin of the pork with a very sharp knife – a Stanley knife works really well or ask your butcher to do this for you. Pick the leaves from the thyme and rub them into the pork with the salt and pepper, ensuring you get plenty of seasoning into the slashes. Drizzle a little olive oil over the rind and rub it in well with your hands. This will ensure crisp crackling.

Place the apple quarters in the centre of a roasting tray, lay the pork on top and roast for 30–35 minutes. Reduce the temperature to 180°C and roast the pork for 1 hour. Check the temperature of the meat using a thermometer – the inside temperature should be 70–75°C.

When ready, the pork will have terrific (and very nibble-able) crackling. The meat should be just cooked and juicy. Allow the pork to rest for 30 minutes before carving.

Make gravy as for Roast Beef (opposite), including the apples as a base. You can use good dry cider instead of red wine.

Roast Lamb

Lamb has got to be my favourite red meat. I love its slight gaminess and distinctive flavour. Local lamb is at its best, in my opinion, in late spring and summer when it has had a little more time to mature.

1 leg of lamb

small bunch of rosemary

3 bulbs of garlic

salt and freshly ground black pepper

olive oil for cooking

2 onions, halved

2 carrots, halved lengthways

3–4 celery sticks

2 bay leaves

Gravy

½ bottle red wine

425ml lamb stock

2–3 tsp redcurrant jelly

SERVES 6–8

Preheat the oven to 210°C.

Using a sharp, pointed knife, make 15–20 small slits, about 3cm deep, all over the lamb. Bruise the rosemary by whacking it with the back of a knife a few times and then break it into small sprigs. Squeeze the sprigs into the holes in the lamb. Remove the cloves from 2 of the bulbs of garlic, peel the cloves, cut them across into 2mm slices and then lengthways into slivers. Push these slivers of garlic into the holes with the rosemary. Season the lamb well with salt and pepper and rub in some olive oil.

Heat a roasting tin over medium heat. Add a little olive oil and then the leg of lamb. Brown the meat well on all sides, remove it from the tin and set to one side.

Slice the remaining bulb of garlic in half horizontally. Using more olive oil, if necessary, brown the vegetables and halved bulb of garlic in the same tin until they have softened slightly and taken on some colour. Bring all the vegetables to the centre of the tin, tuck in the bay leaves and any leftover rosemary and place the lamb on top.

Roast the lamb for 15 minutes, then reduce the oven temperature to 180°C. It's a good idea to baste the lamb with the cooking juices at this point. Continue roasting for a further 1–1¼ hours, depending on the size of the lamb leg. Test the meat's temperature with a thermometer – it should be at least 60°C in the middle for medium, or 70–75°C for a well-cooked joint.

When it's cooked, allow the lamb to rest for about 30 minutes. In the meantime, you can make the gravy. Drain as much fat as possible from the tin, leaving the meat juices and vegetables. Place the tin over medium heat and pour in the red wine. Bring to the boil. Stir well to dislodge all the caramelised meat juices from the bottom of the pan and try to squeeze the garlic flesh out of the cloves – this will help to flavour the gravy. When the wine has reduced by half, add the stock and continue to reduce. Finally, add the redcurrant jelly and stir well. Strain the gravy into a jug or gravy boat and you're ready to go.

Confit of Duck

Try these duck legs with with Creamed Celeriac Mash (page 102), steamed green vegetables and redcurrant gravy. They're also perfect with Flageolet Bean Stew (page 99). Whichever way you choose, and whatever you choose to serve them with, they are absolute food heaven.

4 tbsp rock salt

6 garlic cloves, roughly chopped

1 tsp ground cumin

1 tsp cracked black peppercorns

3 tsp roughly chopped thyme

8 duck legs, thigh bones removed

1kg duck or goose fat

SERVES 4

Mix the salt with the garlic, cumin, peppercorns and thyme. Rub this mixture all over the duck legs, concentrating especially on the flesh side of the legs where the thigh bones have been removed. Place the duck legs in a dish, cover with clingfilm and chill for 24 hours.

Preheat the oven to 150°C.

Gently melt the goose fat in a large pan or deep roasting tin. Brush off as much of the salt mixture as you can from the duck legs, but do not wash them. Place the duck legs in the tin and ensure they are completely submerged in fat – top it up if necessary. Place in the oven for 3– 3½ hours, by which time the duck legs should be extremely tender. Remove from the oven and allow to cool a little.

Remove the legs from their cooking container and place in a sterilised crock, kilner or other preserving jar. Strain the fat through a fine sieve and pour it over the legs: again, ensure they are completely submerged in fat. Cover the crock or close the jar and allow to cool to room temperature before chilling. The duck confit will keep unopened for up to 6 months in the fridge, as long as the legs are completely submerged in fat.

To cook, preheat the oven to 200°C. Place the duck legs on a trivet in a roasting tin and blast in the oven for 25 minutes or until the skin is crisp and the duck legs are thoroughly heated through. Retain the fat to use for your next batches – you can use it twice or three times more.

Pan-seared Barbary Duck Fillets with Leafy Greens, Pomegranates and Pomegranate Molasses Dressing

In this delicious salad, the freshness of the pomegranate seeds perfectly counteracts the richness of the duck. You can buy pomegranate molasses in Asian supermarkets.

4 boneless Barbary duck breasts

salt and freshly ground black pepper

4 handfuls bitter salad leaves, such as frisée, young beetroot leaves, mizuna or chicory

seeds from ½ pomegranate

Dressing

2 tbsp pomegranate molasses

4 tbsp extra-virgin olive oil

2 tbsp chopped coriander leaves

grated zest and juice of ½ orange

SERVES 4

Remove any sinew from the back of the duck breasts. Score the skin side at 5mm intervals and season thoroughly.

Heat a frying pan over high heat and, without adding any oil, fry the fillets skin-side down. After 2 minutes, reduce the heat to medium-low and continue to cook for another 2–3 minutes, then turn the fillets over and cook for a further couple of minutes. Don't be tempted to move or turn the fillets any sooner. Remove from the heat and set aside to rest.

To make the dressing, mix the molasses, oil, coriander, orange zest and juice, and seasoning. Divide the salad leaves among four serving bowls and sprinkle the pomegranate seeds over. Carve the duck fillets lengthways and place on top of the salad. Drizzle the dressing over and serve.

Barbecued Spare Ribs

I have always wondered where spare ribs got their name and guess that before barbecues they weren't just as popular, so butchers christened them 'spare' as they may have been hard to sell. Spare or not, they are quite delicious. I prefer to simmer mine for a little while before coating with sauce and barbecuing or grilling. This ensures they are really tender underneath the charred, sweet and spicy flavour that is so delicious. The sauce can be made in advance and kept in the fridge for up to 7 days.

1kg sheet of rare-breed pork ribs

2 stalks each of parsley, rosemary, thyme and sage, tied tightly together with string

1 cinnamon stick

50g butter

50ml olive oil

2 onions, finely chopped

4 garlic cloves, finely chopped

1 tsp chilli powder or dried chilli flakes

½ tsp ground cumin

½ tsp ground cloves

1 tsp paprika

3 tbsp cider vinegar or white wine vinegar

4 tbsp dark brown sugar

100ml honey

juice of ½ lemon

300ml tomato ketchup

2 tbsp Worcestershire sauce

salt and freshly ground black pepper

SERVES 2, OR 4 AS A FIRST COURSE

Place the ribs in a large saucepan with the tied herbs and cinnamon stick. Pour in water to cover, bring to the boil, reduce the heat and simmer for 45–60 minutes.

Meanwhile, prepare the sauce. Melt the butter in a saucepan with the olive oil. Add the onions and cook until well browned. Add the garlic, chilli powder or flakes, cumin, cloves and paprika and cook for a further 1–2 minutes. Pour in the vinegar, sugar and honey and stir to dissolve the sugar. Add the honey, lemon juice, tomato ketchup, Worcestershire sauce and seasoning and simmer over low heat for 45 minutes.

The sauce and ribs should be ready at about the same time. Take the ribs out of the water (the water, or stock, makes a great base for soups, so don't throw it away) and transfer to a large shallow dish. Allow them to cool for a little while before coating them with the sauce. Leave the ribs to marinate in the sauce for 2 hours.

Preheat a grill or prepare the barbecue. Grill the ribs until well browned on both sides and serve immediately.

Roast Pork Belly with Roasties

Belly of pork is one of my favourite cuts of meat. It is inexpensive and bursting with flavour. I prefer to cook it long and slow as this helps to extract some of the fat and ensures 'cut with a spoon' tenderness. As an American chef once told me, 'Long and slow is the way to go'.

1.5–2kg pork belly, skin on

2 onions, cut into chunks

2 carrots, cut into chunks

2 bay leaves

3–4 parsley stalks

2 thyme or sage sprigs

1 garlic bulb, halved horizontally

sea salt and freshly ground black pepper

olive oil for cooking

10 large floury potatoes, quartered

1 large glass of dry cider

SERVES 6–8

Preheat the oven to 220°C.

Score the skin of the pork at 1cm intervals, to a depth of around 5mm, with a very sharp knife (a Stanley knife works really well, or ask your butcher to do this for you).

Place the onions and carrots in the middle of a large roasting tin and put the bay leaves, parsley, thyme or sage, and garlic on top. Lightly season the flesh side of the pork belly. Turn it over, massage a little olive oil into the skin side and season again, more heavily on this side. Use the tips of your fingers to work the seasoning into the slits in the skin. Place the pork on top of the vegetables, skin-side up, and then roast in the oven for 15 minutes.

Meanwhile, boil the potatoes in salted water for about 10 minutes to cook them a little and soften their edges. Drain the potatoes, return them to the pan and dry them out over a low heat, shaking the pan occasionally to dry the surface of the potatoes and to rough up their edges a little. This will ensure lovely, crisp roasties.

Take the pork out of the oven and place the potatoes around it, rolling them thoroughly in the cooking juices. The skin of the pork should be starting to crisp up.

Roast the pork and potatoes for a further 30 minutes, until the pork skin is beginning to get very crisp, then reduce the oven temperature to 185°C and roast for a further 45 minutes to 1 hour, turning the potatoes occasionally. Check that the pork is cooked through – when pierced, the juices should run clear (or use a meat thermometer – it should reach 75°C). Transfer the meat to a large platter, cover it loosely with foil and allow to rest. Remove the potatoes from the roasting tray. They should be crisp and nicely browned. Place the potatoes back in the oven on a separate tray and turn the oven off.

To make the gravy, pour off any excess fat from the roasting tin. Place the tin over medium heat and add the cider. Bring to the boil, stirring constantly to get all the nice crispy bits off the bottom of the tray. Squeeze the sweet roast garlic into the gravy. When the cider has reduced by about a third, strain the gravy into a clean pan and discard the vegetables and herbs.

You are now ready to plate up. Carve the pork belly into thick slices (about 2.5cm) and serve with the roasties. Steamed green vegetables, such as chard, cabbage or broccoli, are good with the pork too. Pour over the cider gravy and enjoy.

Lamb Shanks with Prunes

I like to serve this with wet polenta to mop up the intensely flavoured liquor, or you can also serve it with puréed potatoes for a more traditional meal. Boil the potatoes in the usual way, until soft, then add milk and butter, and whip up with a hand-held electric whisk. This makes them much lighter than mashing the usual way. Serve some squeaky steamed greens, such as cabbage, alongside for a great contrast.

olive oil for cooking

4 lamb shanks

12 shallots, peeled

100g thick dry-cure streaky bacon rashers, diced

2 garlic cloves, chopped

1 bottle Rioja or similar robust red wine

350g prunes

2 tsp juniper berries

handful of thyme sprigs

SERVES 4

Preheat the oven to 170°C.

Heat a little oil in a heavy-bottomed ovenproof casserole over medium-high heat. Cook the lamb shanks in the hot oil, turning regularly so that they brown on all sides. You may have to do this in batches. Once all the lamb shanks are browned, remove them from the casserole and set aside.

Reduce the heat a little and add a splash more oil. Add the shallots and bacon, and cook until the bacon starts to brown at the edges. Add the garlic and cook for about 30 seconds (don't allow it to burn or it will taste bitter). Pop the lamb shanks back into the pot and pour in the wine. Add the prunes and juniper berries, tuck the thyme under the surface of the wine and bring to the boil.

Cover the casserole and place in the oven for 2 hours. Check progress after 1½ hours: the liquid should reduce to a slightly sticky gravy, but should not dry out completely. When cooked, the liquid should be reduced to a quarter of the original volume, but this will depend on how tight-fitting the lid is. If too much liquid has evaporated, add more wine (or stock) but don't reduce the overall cooking time. If the gravy hasn't reduced sufficiently, remove the shanks and reduce the liquid over medium-high heat on the hob for 5–8 minutes, squashing the prunes to help the sauce to thicken. Put the shanks back into the dish to warm through, if necessary.

Serve each shank with a generous spoonful of sauce over the top.

Shepherd's Pie with Root Vegetable Mash

I have included this classic but delicious recipe to highlight the method we use for cooking many of our meat and vegetable pies. The two-pan method speeds up the cooking process and, more importantly, caramelises the vegetables and meat, which improves the appearance and colour of the pie filling, and naturally sweetens the dish.

Filling

olive oil for cooking

180g flat-cap mushrooms, diced

2 onions, diced

2 carrots, diced

2 celery sticks, diced

2 garlic cloves, finely chopped

knob of butter

450g minced Irish lamb

1½ tbsp tomato purée

1½ tbsp Worcestershire sauce

2 bay leaves

small bunch of rosemary, thyme and flat-leaf parsley, finely chopped

550ml lamb or beef stock

salt and freshly ground black pepper

Topping

8 floury potatoes, peeled and cut into even-sized pieces

2 carrots, roughly diced

2 small parsnips, roughly diced

100g butter

salt and freshly ground white pepper

SERVES 6

Prepare the filling: heat a large saucepan and a frying pan over high heat. Add a good splash of olive oil to each pan. Fry the mushrooms in the saucepan and the onions in the frying pan. The onions will cook more quickly than the mushrooms, so when they start to colour, add them to the mushrooms in the saucepan and continue cooking. Add the carrots and celery to the frying pan, with a little more olive oil if necessary, and cook until they begin to soften. Turn the heat down a little if you think anything is cooking too quickly. Transfer the carrot and celery to the saucepan, and add the garlic and butter. Continue to cook, stirring occasionally.

Meanwhile, brown the lamb in batches in the frying pan. Don't overcrowd the pan – the meat should fry rather than stew in its juices. When each batch is starting to brown, tip it into the saucepan. Add the tomato purée, Worcestershire sauce, herbs, stock and seasoning to the meat mixture. Stir well and reduce the heat so that the filling simmers gently while you get on with making the topping.

Preheat the oven to 180°C.

Cook the potatoes in boiling salted water until tender. Drain and dry out over very low heat for about 5 minutes. While the potatoes are cooking, place the carrots and parsnips in a roasting tin. Drizzle with a little oil and season. Cover loosely with foil and bake for 25 minutes or until tender. Add the roasted vegetables to the potatoes and mash well, adding the butter and seasoning. The mash does not have to be smooth – this is a rustic dish and a little texture will do no harm.

Remove the bay leaves from the lamb filling and pour it into an ovenproof dish. Spread the mash on top, and rough up the surface using a fork – the bits that stick up will become crunchy in the oven. Turn the oven up to 200°C and bake the pie for 25 minutes, until it is is golden brown and crisp on top.

Steak

Before you cook a really nice piece of fillet, rib-eye or sirloin you firstly have to purchase it – easier said than done. I suggest starting with your local butcher: he will be able to advise you on the best cut for the dish you are planning, and should be able to give you lots of information on the provenance of the meat, how long it has been hung for and so on.

The steak you get should be slightly brown, even purple, and should have a slightly (I know it sounds strange) rubbery feel – not wet or dry.

1 steak
salt and pepper
groundnut oil
knob of butter

Heat a frying pan over high heat. Turn your extractor fan on full as cooking a steak is sure to generate a lot of smoke. Smear a little oil over both sides of the steak and season it quite heavily on one side, rubbing the salt and pepper into the meat.

When, and only when, the pan is leaping hot, add the steak, seasoned side down, and cook it for at least 1½ minutes. Season the steak carefully before turning it over. Cook for another minute or so. You may add a little more oil at this stage if the pan looks dry.

Reduce the heat a little and add a nice fat knob of butter (weighing about 40g). Using a spoon, baste the steak with the melted butter until it is cooked to your liking.

Contrary to common Irish belief, a rare prime cut steak will always be far more tender than a well-done one. This is because the protein in the meat will contract and toughen during grilling or frying, so the more you cook it the harder and dryer it will become. If you employ a slow, moist cooking method, the protein and connective tissue will eventually break down, but this takes a couple of hours.

The other important thing to remember when you go to a restaurant is that the well-done steak will end up smaller than the rare one, even if they start out at the same raw weight. This is because of the moisture loss during cooking. I would encourage 'well doners' to try your steak medium at least, to experience a more juicy, flavoursome and tender piece of meat.

Béarnaise Sauce

The very mention of béarnaise or hollandaise strikes fear into the hearts of all but the bravest or most confident of home cooks. In this recipe, however, I've made things easier: I do not clarify the butter but instead add it in dice. This way you have a much better chance of not shouting at your stove and obtaining a really velvety rich sauce. It's delicious with steak (opposite), salmon and poured over poached eggs.

120ml cider or white wine vinegar

2 shallots, finely chopped

8–10 black peppercorns

1 bunch of tarragon

4 egg yolks

250g butter, cut into 25mm cubes

squeeze of lemon juice

Place the vinegar, shallots, peppercorns and tarragon stalks (retaining the leaves) into a small saucepan and boil to reduce. When the vinegar has almost all evaporated, add a dessertspoon of water, remove from the heat and strain the liquid into a stainless steel bowl.

Chop the tarragon leaves. Place the egg yolks into the bowl and place the bowl over a pot of barely boiling water ensuring the base of the bowl is not in contact with the boiling water. Whisk the eggs and vinegar continuously until the egg foam stiffens slightly and the mixture can just about hold a figure of eight.

If you find the egg is cooking too quickly, remove the bowl from the pot and continue whisking.

Now that the egg has stiffened add the butter, a couple of knobs at a time, ensuring each addition has melted and been incorporated into the mix before you add the next knobs.

When all the butter has been incorporated remove from the heat, add a squeeze of lemon juice and the tarragon leaves. The sauce is ready to serve immediately or you can keep it warm until you are ready to eat.

End of the Meal

Puff Pastry Apple Pie / Maple Syrup and Nutmeg Ice Cream / Vanilla Ice Cream / Coconut Ice Cream / Griddled Pineapple with Basil and Raspberries / Pistachio and Olive Oil Cake / Ricotta Pancakes / Pain Perdu with Roasted Apricots / Sauternes-poached Figs with Rosewater Mascarpone / Chocolate and Bailey's Bread and Butter Pudding / Victoria Plum Clafoutis Tart / Yellowman and Mascarpone Cheesecake with Chocolate Sauce /Rhubarb Galette / Flourless Chocolate Cake / Raspberry Crème Brûlée / Passionfruit Vacherin / Summer Pudding / Strawberry Sorbet / Armagh Strawberry Mascarpone Tart with Chocolate Pastry / Cheese, Honey and Nuts / Yellowman / Home-made Chocolate Truffles

Puff Pastry Apple Pie

This pie differs from classic apple pie because it uses puff pastry instead of shortcrust and includes a small amount of cornflour in the apple mix. This American technique thickens the apples' cooking juices. Try the Maple Syrup and Nutmeg Ice Cream (opposite) with this pie. It's delicious with apples, but you can be brave and substitute other fruits that are in season, such as rhubarb or gooseberries, for the apples.

25g unsalted butter, softened

800g Bramley apples, peeled, cored and roughly chopped

6 cloves

juice of 1 lemon

150g caster sugar

1 tbsp cornflour

375g puff pastry

1–2 tbsp milk

SERVES 8–10

Preheat the oven to 180°C. Use the butter to grease a loose-bottomed tart tin, 20cm in diameter and 5cm in depth.

In a large bowl, mix together the apples, cloves, lemon juice, 125g of the sugar and cornflour. Set aside.

Roll out two-thirds of the pastry large enough to line the base and sides of the tart tin, allowing some overhang. Gently line the tin, and then spoon in the apple mixture, spreading out the cloves if they have bunched together. Brush a little water around the edges. Roll out the final third of pastry and place it over the top of the tart. With your fingers, pinch the pastry together around the edge to form a seal. Cut off any excess with a sharp knife.

Brush the top of the tart with milk and sprinkle the remaining sugar evenly over it. Make four small incisions in the lid and bake the pie for 25 minutes.

After 25 minutes, reduce the oven temperature to 150°C and continue to bake for a further 40–45 minutes. Remove from oven and leave to cool for 30 minutes before serving.

Variations

If using rhubarb, substitute the finely grated zest of ½ orange for the cloves. If you go for gooseberries, add 5 finely chopped pieces of stem ginger instead of the cloves.

Maple Syrup and Nutmeg Ice Cream

I discovered this ice cream by accident, really – just by playing with flavours that work well together. It's especially good with the apple pie (opposite) but, like all ice cream, it's equally delicious on its own.

500ml double cream

200ml milk

200ml condensed milk

2 vanilla pods, split lengthways and seeds scraped out

5 cloves

100ml maple syrup

1 bay leaf

1 tsp freshly grated nutmeg

5 egg yolks

30g caster sugar

MAKES APPROXIMATELY 1 LITRE

Mix the cream, milk, condensed milk, vanilla seeds, cloves, maple syrup, bay leaf and nutmeg in a saucepan and place over medium heat. Bring to the boil, then take off the heat and leave to one side to allow the flavours to infuse for at least 15 minutes.

Using a hand-held electric beater, whisk the egg yolks and sugar together in a large bowl until very pale and the consistency of whipped cream. This should take about 4 minutes.

Pour the hot cream mixture through a fine sieve onto the egg mixture and stir until well combined. Pour the custard into a clean saucepan and heat gently, stirring constantly, until it starts to thicken. Be careful not to overheat the custard as the eggs will curdle if they get too hot. Leave to cool.

Once the mixture has cooled, pour it through a fine sieve into an ice cream maker and churn according to the manufacturer's instructions. Alternatively, strain it into a plastic container and freeze. Every 30 minutes, break up the ice crystals by whisking the mixture. The ice cream should be ready in about 2 hours. Remove it from the freezer at least 20 minutes before you want to serve it.

Vanilla Ice Cream

300ml milk

300ml double cream

2 vanilla pods, split lengthways and seeds scraped out

6 egg yolks

100g sugar

MAKES APPROXIMATELY 750ML

Place the milk, cream and vanilla seeds in a pan and heat gently. Do not allow to boil.

Using an electric hand-held beater, whisk the egg yolks and sugar together in a large bowl until very pale and the consistency of whipped cream. This should take about 4 minutes. Gradually pour the hot cream mixture over the eggs, stirring constantly.

Pour the custard back into a clean saucepan and heat gently, stirring constantly, until it starts to thicken. Be careful not to overheat the custard or it will curdle. Leave to cool.

Once the mixture has cooled, pour it through a fine sieve into an ice cream maker and churn it according to the manufacturer's instructions. Alternatively, strain it into a plastic container and freeze. Every 30 minutes, break up the ice crystals by whisking the mixture. The ice cream should be ready in about 2 hours. Remove from the freezer at least 20 minutes before you want to eat.

Coconut Ice Cream

This ice cream is wonderful with the Griddled Pineapple with Basil and Raspberries (page 128).

350ml milk

350ml double cream

300ml coconut milk

8 egg yolks

250g caster sugar

75g desiccated coconut

MAKES APPROXIMATELY 1.25 LITRES

Heat the milk, cream and coconut milk in a saucepan over medium heat. Bring up to the boil, then take off the heat and leave to one side to allow the flavours to infuse for about 15 minutes.

Using an electric hand-held beater, whisk the eggs and sugar together in a large bowl until very pale and the consistency of whipped cream. This should take about 4 minutes.

Pour the cream mixture onto the egg mixture and stir until well combined. Pour this custard into a clean saucepan and heat gently, stirring constantly, until it is just thick enough to coat the back of a spoon. Be careful not to overheat the custard as it will curdle. Strain into a bowl and mix in the desiccated coconut. Leave to cool.

Transfer the cool coconut mixture to an ice cream machine and churn it, according to the manufacturer's instructions. This is a large quantity of ice cream so you may need to churn it in two batches. Alternatively, strain it into a plastic container and freeze, breaking up the ice crystals about every 30 minutes by whisking the mixture. The ice cream should be ready in about 2 hours. Remove it from the freezer at least 20 minutes before you want to serve it.

Griddled Pineapple with Basil and Raspberries

To make summer magic, try this with Coconut Ice Cream (page 127).

3 tbsp icing sugar

½ tsp freshly ground black pepper

1 ripe pineapple, peeled, cored and cut lengthways into 8 wedges

75g unsalted butter

75ml golden rum

bunch of basil

200g raspberries

SERVES 4

Sift 1 tablespoon of the icing sugar onto a flat plate. Mix in the black pepper and the roll the pineapple wedges in the mixture.

Heat a deep-sided griddle or frying pan over high heat. Add the pineapple wedges and cook until they are lightly coloured on all sides. Turn the heat down to medium and add the butter and rum so that a caramel syrup will start to form. Turn the heat down to low, throw in the basil leaves and leave for 1 minute, long enough for the basil to wilt.

Meanwhile, in a separate saucepan, heat the raspberries with about 2 tablespoonfuls of water and the remaining icing sugar. Bring to the boil, turn the heat down and stir gently until the icing sugar has dissolved, trying not to break down the raspberries too much.

To serve, place 2 wedges of pineapple on each plate. Drizzle over a little of the basil syrup and spoon over the warm raspberries. Serve with a generous scoop of coconut ice cream.

Pistachio and Olive Oil Cake

You need a light olive oil for this recipe, rather than a strongly flavoured extra-virgin oil.

50g polenta, plus extra for the cake tin

50g plain flour

200g unsalted shelled pistachios

1 tsp baking powder

125ml olive oil

100g unsalted butter, melted and cooled, plus extra for greasing the tin

3 large eggs

200g caster sugar

grated zest of 2 lemons and juice of 1 lemon

grated zest and juice of 1 orange

SERVES 8–10

Preheat the oven to 160°C. Grease a 23cm loose-bottomed cake tin with butter. Sprinkle in some polenta and roll it around the tin to coat the sides. Add more polenta if necessary, then shake out any excess.

Sift the flour into a bowl. Add the polenta, pistachios and baking powder. In a separate bowl or jug, mix the olive oil and melted butter together.

Using a hand-held electric beater, whisk the eggs and sugar together until pale in colour and more than doubled in volume – this should take about 3 minutes. Slowly drizzle in the oil and butter, whisking all the time. Whisk in the flour mixture and, when combined, mix in the citrus zest and juice.

Pour the cake mixture into the prepared tin and bake for about 40 minutes. The cake should be very slightly undercooked when removed from the oven: to check this, place a metal skewer into the middle and if it comes out with a little mixture on it, then all to the good. The cooling process will complete the cooking, creating a moist cake. Serve warm or at room temperature with Sauternes-poached Figs with Rosewater Mascarpone (page 134).

Ricotta Pancakes

The perfect summer barbecue dessert. If you prefer, substitute an orange for the lemon. My favourite way of serving these is with warm strawberries (see below).

250g ricotta cheese

4 tbsp caster sugar

3 eggs, separated

grated zest of 1 lemon

50g plain flour

2 tbsp unsalted butter

SERVES 4–6

In a large mixing bowl, combine the ricotta, caster sugar, egg yolks and lemon zest. Sift in the flour and stir gently to mix.

In a separate bowl, whisk the egg whites until stiff. Fold the egg whites into the ricotta using a spatula, trying not to knock out the air. The whisked whites give the pancakes their delicious, light texture.

Melt the butter in a non-stick frying pan and, just as it starts to sizzle, add a heaped tablespoon of the ricotta mixture. Depending on the size of the pan, you should be able to cook 3–4 pancakes at a time, but, beware, they will spread to about 8 cm. Cook the pancakes for about 1–1½ minutes, then turn them over and cook for another 1–1½ minutes on the other side. They should be slightly 'unset' in the middle. Serve immediately.

Serving suggestions

Blueberries or raspberries
Place 100g blueberries or raspberries in a pan with some sugar to taste, 2 tablespoons water and the juice of ½ lemon. Heat gently until the berries start to break down. Serve with the pancakes.

Lemon curd and yoghurt
Mix together lemon curd into some greek yoghurt, to taste, and spoon over the pancakes while still warm.

Strawberries
Melt 50g unsalted butter in a frying pan and, when sizzling, add about 20 strawberries, 50g caster sugar and a little black pepper. Cook for 2 minutes – you want to the strawberries to hold their shape. Serve with the pancakes.

Pain Perdu with Roasted Apricots

The essential accompaniment for this recipe is very well chilled pudding wine.

4 x 2.5cm thick slices brioche

4 egg yolks

100g unrefined sugar

250ml semi-skimmed milk

250ml double cream

12 fresh apricots

2 rosemary sprigs

1 bay leaf

2 star anise

grated zest of 1 lemon

1 vanilla pod, split lengthways and seeds scraped out

2 tbsp orange blossom honey

100ml boiling water

200g unsalted butter

Vanilla Ice Cream (page 126), to serve

SERVES 4

Preheat the oven to 180°C. Allow the slices of brioche to dry out a little at room temperature while you prepare the rest of the dish.

Make the egg custard by whisking the eggs and sugar with a hand-held electric beater in a large bowl until they have increased in volume, become very pale and are the consistency of whipped cream. This should take about 3 minutes.

Heat the milk and cream together in a saucepan until almost boiling – watch closely, and don't allow the mixture to boil. Pour the mixture onto the yolks, stirring all the time until smooth. Leave to cool. You aren't aiming for traditional custard here, which is why you don't need to cook the mixture until it thickens. You're going to use this custard to soak the brioche before pan frying – like French toast, but sweet rather than savoury.

Halve the apricots vertically and remove their stone. Place them in a roasting tin, cut-side up. Tuck the rosemary sprigs, bay leaf and star anise among the apricots. Sprinkle over the lemon zest.

Place the vanilla seeds and honey in a separate bowl. (You can dry the vanilla pod after this and place it in your sugar jar: the scent of the vanilla will slowly permeate all the sugar.) Pour in the boiling water, stirring to melt the honey. Mix well and pour the mixture over the apricots.

Bake the apricots for about 15 minutes. The apricots should be soft but still holding their shape – it's vital that they don't turn to mush! The cooking time will depend upon the ripeness of the fruit, so keep checking. Remove the rosemary, bay leaf and star anise.

Dip the brioche slices into the cooled custard. They will absorb it quite dramatically. Soak each slice only when you're ready to cook it otherwise the bread will disintegrate if left in the custard for too long.

Melt the butter in a frying pan over medium heat. Once the butter has started to foam, add the brioche. Fry on the first side until golden brown. Then turn using a fish slice and cook until the other side is the same colour. Don't let the butter burn or it will become bitter. Repeat the process until you have 4 amber-coloured brioche slices.

To serve, put a slice of brioche into the centre of each plate. Place 6 apricot halves on each slice of brioche, and spoon over a little syrup from the roasting tin. Place a scoop of vanilla ice cream on top and serve.

Sauternes-poached Figs with Rosewater Mascarpone

Figs are one of those fruits people aren't sure what to do with. Believe me, they are delicious and this recipe makes a lavish dessert.

200ml Sauternes (and a well chilled glass for the chef!)

2 dsp unrefined caster sugar

juice of ½ lemon

1 vanilla pod, split lengthways and seeds scraped out

6 ripe figs, halved

Rosewater mascarpone

150g mascarpone

50ml double cream, lightly whipped

2–3 tsp rosewater

SERVES 4

Mix the mascarpone, softly whipped cream and rosewater together in a bowl. Chill until you are ready to serve.

Heat the Sauternes, sugar and lemon juice in a large deep frying pan over medium heat. Add the seeds from the vanilla pod and bring to a gentle simmer. Add the fig halves and allow to cook gently for about 2 minutes on each side. The figs will not be completely submerged in the liquid. Remove the figs from the poaching liquor. Turn up the heat and simmer for 4–5 minutes, until reduced and syrupy.

To serve, place 3 fig halves on each plate. Add a dollop of the mascarpone and drizzle over the Sauternes syrup.

Chocolate and Bailey's Bread and Butter Pudding

This dessert is best eaten fresh, not reheated, but I don't think you'll have any leftovers to worry about, anyway!

1 small Brioche loaf

100g unsalted butter

500ml milk

500ml double cream

6 eggs

3 egg yolks

175g caster sugar

100g best quality plain chocolate (at least 60% cocoa solids), chopped

2 good measures of Bailey's Irish Cream liqueur

icing sugar, to caramelise

Vanilla Ice Cream (page 126), to serve

SERVES 6

Slice the brioche and butter each slice generously with unsalted butter.

Heat the milk and cream in a saucepan to just below boiling point. Do not allow it to boil over. Place the eggs, yolks and sugar in a bowl and whisk, using a hand-held electric beater, until light in colour and frothy – this should take about 3 minutes. Whisk in half the hot milk and cream. Once it is mixed in, add the remaining milk and cream. This method ensures that the eggs do not curdle.

Add 65g of the chocolate to the hot mixture and allow to melt, stirring occasionally. Stir in the Bailey's.

Halve the brioche slices and arrange them, overlapping, in an ovenproof dish. Sprinkle the remaining chocolate over the brioche. Using a fine sieve, strain the custard into the dish. Allow the brioche to stand and absorb the liquid for 25 minutes.

Preheat oven to 180°C.

Bake the pudding for 20–25 minutes, until the custard has just set. Dust the top of the pudding with icing sugar and use a blowtorch to caramelise the top. Serve warm, with lots of vanilla ice cream.

Victoria Plum Clafoutis Tart

This simple dessert is hearty and comforting, especially with ice cream or a gallon of custard. You can replace the plums with other soft fruit in season and at its best – why not try raspberries, cherries, peaches, nectarines or strawberries?

Sweet pastry

180g flour, plus extra for dusting

125g butter, plus extra for greasing

50g caster sugar

1 egg yolk

10 ripe Victoria plums, halved and stoned

60g plain flour

90g caster sugar

2 eggs – lightly beaten

200ml milk

50g butter, melted

1 tsp vanilla extract

icing sugar, for dusting

SERVES 12

To make the pastry, sift the flour into a bowl, rub in the butter until the mixture resembles fine breadcrumbs and stir in the sugar. Use a knife to mix in the egg yolk, then gently press the mixture together, using your hands. Wrap in clingfilm and allow to rest for at least 1 hour in the fridge.

Preheat the oven to 200°C. Lightly grease a deep, 30cm wide, loose-bottomed flan tin.

Roll out the pastry on a lightly floured surface, large enough to line the base and sides of the flan tin. Roll the pastry over a rolling pin to lift it into the tin. Press it into the bottom, allowing a little to hang over the rim of the tin. Arrange the plum halves around the base of the tin, cut-side up.

Mix the flour and caster sugar in a bowl. Add the eggs, milk, butter and vanilla extract. Beat the mixture, using a whisk, to make a smooth batter. Pour the batter into the tin, trying not to disturb the positioning of the plums.

Bake the tart for about 40 minutes, until the top is golden brown. If, during cooking, it seems to be browning too quickly, cover loosely with foil. Remove from the oven and dust with icing sugar.

Yellowman and Mascarpone Cheesecake with Chocolate Sauce

Hardly a recipe for anyone who is weight-watching, but delicious nonetheless.

100g digestive or gingernut biscuits, crushed

75g unsalted butter, melted

2 gelatine leaves

225g mascarpone

1 tsp vanilla extract

2 egg whites

70g extra-fine caster sugar

325ml whipping cream, softly whipped

75g yellowman, crushed (page 154)

Chocolate sauce

100g plain chocolate (at least 60% cocoa solids), chopped

75ml whipping cream

SERVES 8–10

Preheat the oven to 190°C.

To make the base, mix the biscuits and butter in a bowl. Tip the mixture into a 20cm round loose-bottomed cake tin and press down well. Bake for 6–8 minutes to ensure that the base stays crisp. Set aside to cool.

Soak the gelatine in a bowl of cold water for about 15 minutes. Remove the gelatine from the water and squeeze it to remove excess water. Place the gelatine in a small bowl with 3 tablespoons of boiling water and stir until it has dissolved completely.

Meanwhile, mix the mascarpone and vanilla extract in a large bowl and beat with a wooden spoon to soften. In another (perfectly clean) bowl, whisk the egg whites until they form soft peaks. Add the sugar and whisk briefly again to mix. Set aside.

Beat the dissolved gelatine into the mascarpone. Mix in the lightly whipped cream. Sprinkle in the crushed Yellowman and add half the egg whites. Fold gently with a spatula until mixed, and then fold in the remaining egg whites. Spoon the mascarpone topping over the base, spread it evenly and chill for at least 4 hours, or preferably overnight.

To prepare the chocolate sauce, place the chocolate in a heatproof bowl. Heat the cream until it's just coming up to the boil, then pour it over the chocolate and stir until the chocolate has completely melted.

Serve the cheesecake with the warm, rich chocolate sauce. The chocolate sauce will set when cool, but can easily be warmed through in a microwave.

Rhubarb Galette

375g puff pastry

160g Frangipane (page 9)

3 rhubarb stalks

50g butter, melted

80g brown sugar

grated zest of 1 orange

2cm piece fresh root ginger, peeled and finely grated

SERVES 4

Preheat the oven to 190°C.

Roll out the puff pastry to a thickness of around 4mm. Cut out four circles, measuring approximately 14cm – use a saucer as a template if you wish. Prick the pastry all over with a fork, then spread a thin layer of frangipane over the surface of each pastry circle. Lay the circles on a baking sheet.

Slice the rhubarb, at an angle of 45°, into 10mm slices. Lay the slices on top of the frangipane in overlapping circles until the whole surface is covered. Repeat for the other tarts.

Brush the rhubarb with melted butter and sprinkle over the sugar (you may need extra if the rhubarb is particularly bitter), orange zest and ginger. Bake for 25 minutes and serve immediately with Vanilla Ice Cream (page 126).

Flourless Chocolate Cake

This chocolate cake is delicious, and surprisingly light given the amount of chocolate in the recipe. To those chocoholics suffering from gluten intolerance, this is also known as coeliac heaven.

melted butter, for greasing

275g plain chocolate (at least 60% cocoa solids)

185g unsalted butter

200g caster sugar

7 eggs, separated

150g ground almonds

150g ground hazelnuts

1 tsp baking powder

To serve and decorate

icing sugar

mint sprigs

raspberries

whipped cream

Preheat the oven to 170°C. Lightly grease a 23cm round loose-bottomed cake tin with melted butter.

Melt the chocolate in a heatproof bowl over a pan of simmering water. Don't allow the bowl to come into contact with the water. When melted, set the chocolate to one side.

Beat the butter and sugar together with a hand-held electric beater until light and creamy. Add the egg yolks, one at a time, incorporating each one into the mixture before adding the next. Fold in the melted chocolate and ground almonds and hazelnuts, and sift in the baking powder.

Whisk the egg whites in a clean bowl until they are fluffy and form soft peaks. Using a spatula or metal spoon, fold half the egg whites into the chocolate mixture. When incorporated, add the remaining egg whites and fold in, working gently to retain the lightness of the mix.

Pour the mixture into the prepared tin and smooth the top lightly with the back of a spoon or spatula. Bake for 50–60 minutes. To check whether the cake is cooked, insert a skewer into the middle. If it comes out clean, or with just a little mixture on it, the cake is cooked.

Allow the cake to cool in the tin before turning out. Dust with icing sugar, and top with fresh local raspberries and sprigs of mint. Serve with extra raspberries and whipped cream on the side.

Raspberry Crème Brûlée

Crème brûlée has always been one of our deli favourites, much to the delight of my wife. In fact, prior to our engagement bringing home one of these lovelies at night after work was, I believe, a huge point in my favour, and a big plus in her marriage decision-making process. So, for all you single men out there, here is the secret to a woman's heart.

500ml double cream

1 vanilla pod, split lengthways and seeds scraped out

4 egg yolks

60g caster sugar, plus 8 tsp to glaze

2 small punnets of raspberries (around 36 berries in total)

SERVES 6

Preheat the oven to 160°C.

Place the cream, vanilla pod and seeds in a saucepan. Bring slowly to the boil. Whisk the egg yolks and caster sugar together in a heatproof bowl until light and fluffy. Pour the boiling cream slowly onto the egg mixture, whisking all the time. Strain the mixture through a sieve into a jug. (Retain the vanilla pod for your sugar bowl.)

Divide the raspberries among 6 ramekins, then pour the custard over the top. Place the ramekins in a roasting tin. Pour in warm water to come two-thirds of the way up the outsides of the ramekins and bake for 20–25 minutes, until the custards are almost set. Give them a wobble to check this.

Remove the ramekins from the roasting tin and set aside to cool. Then chill the custards until you are ready to serve them. Sprinkle a teaspoon of caster sugar on top of each one. Spread the sugar out evenly with your finger. Scorch each one with a blowtorch until the sugar is well caramelised – don't worry if it goes a little dark in places. Allow to cool and set a for a few minutes before repeating the process. Be very careful as the sugar on top may still be hot. This double-glazing ensures you get a really crunchy, break-with-the-back-of-a-spoon topping.

Passionfruit Vacherin

This is a great dessert to make if you're having people over as you can make the passionfruit cream and meringue up to 24 hours in advance. Store the meringue in an airtight container and the passionfruit cream in the fridge.

4 egg whites

½ tsp cornflour

475g extra-fine caster sugar

Passionfruit cream

14 passionfruit

150g mascarpone

2 shots of passionfruit liqueur

1 tsp vanilla extract

500ml double cream

4 tbsp icing sugar

SERVES 8

Preheat the oven to 135°C. Line two baking sheets, at least 30cm square, with baking parchment.

Using an electric beater, whisk the egg whites in a very clean bowl, until they form soft peaks. Add the cornflour and half the sugar and continue to whisk the egg whites on high speed until the mixture is stiff and forming sharp peaks. Fold in the remaining sugar.

Fill a large piping bag with the mixture and pipe two discs, about 20cm in diameter, on the lined baking sheets. Bake for 45 minutes. To ensure even cooking, swap the positions of the baking sheets (top to bottom, bottom to top) half way through. Turn off the oven, open the oven door slightly and leave the meringues to dry out and cool.

Reserve two passionfruit for decoration. Remove the pulp from the remaining passionfruit and sieve it, discarding the seeds. Place the pulp in a bowl and mix in the mascarpone, passionfruit liqueur and vanilla extract. In a large bowl, whisk the cream until fairly stiff, sift in the icing sugar and then whisk briefly again to mix thoroughly. Add a third of the cream to the mascarpone mix and stir in, then fold this mixture back into the remaining cream.

To ensure the meringue stays crisp, assemble the dessert no more than 30 minutes before you are ready to serve it. Place one meringue disc on a large round plate and spoon half the cream on top. Flatten the mixture out with the back of the spoon to the edges of the meringue. Place the other disc on top and cover with the remaining cream. Finally, cut the reserved passionfruits in half and scatter the pulp and seeds over the top. Serve immediately.

Summer Pudding

When prepared with local summer berries in season, summer pudding does, truly, epitomise the taste of summer. The reason I have included the recipe in the book is to encourage you to prepare and eat it – it couldn't be easier. In spite of the abundance of strawberries, raspberries and blueberries in summer, you never see this classic pudding on any restaurant menus, which is a great reason to make it yourself.

400g mixed summer berries, plus extra to serve

around 50ml dessert wine, Madeira or sherry

icing sugar to taste

10 slices of white bread, crusts removed and halved lengthways

clotted cream, to serve

SERVES 4

Purée half the berries with the wine in a blender. Taste for sweetness and add a little icing sugar if necessary.

Line four individual pudding moulds, about 150ml capacity each, with clingfilm. I recommend using three or four layers to ensure that the clingfilm goes right down into the edges. Simply place the layers of clingfilm on top of one another on your work surface, flatten and use as normal. (This is a good tip for lining any kind of mould.)

Line each mould with the pieces of bread, first dipping each slice into the purée on one side. Place the dipped sides facing out against the mould. Overlap the slices, and make sure that each mould is completely lined. You should have 4 pieces left to make lids. Give the remaining berries a little crush with the back of a spoon and then divide them among the four moulds.

Spoon about three-quarters of the remaining purée into the moulds, dividing it equally among them. Cut a circle of bread to cover each mould neatly. Dip the circles of bread in the reserved purée before using them to cover the puddings, dipped-side down. Cover the tops of the moulds with clingfilm and place on a tray. Weigh the moulds down with cups or cans, ensuring the puddings are under a little pressure.

Chill for at least 3–4 hours or overnight. Unmould the puddings, remove the clingfilm and serve with clotted cream and extra fresh berries.

Strawberry Sorbet

As with all fruit and vegetable dishes, the fresher the better, so eat your sorbet within a couple of weeks to enjoy the ripe sweet strawberry and fresh mint flavour. It really tastes alive. Always buy fruit from your local supplier – that way you can be sure of getting the best and ripest fruit.

100g caster sugar

120ml water

300g fully ripe strawberries, hulled

juice of ½ lemon

1 tsp finely chopped mint

SERVES 6

Make a sugar syrup by dissolving the sugar in the water in a saucepan over a low heat. Once the sugar has dissolved, set the syrup aside to cool.

Place the strawberries and lemon juice in a blender and blitz to a smooth purée. Mix this purée with the sugar syrup and pass through a fine sieve to remove the seeds. Add the chopped mint.

Pour into an ice cream maker and churn according to the manufacturer's instructions. Place in an airtight container and freeze. Remove from the freezer at least 20 minutes before serving.

Armagh Strawberry Mascarpone Tart with Chocolate Pastry

You can tell this is going to be really good dessert long before you enter your kitchen. Simply smell the first of our local strawberries in spring. Don't bother trying this recipe in December with those giant red forced strawberries – they are more likely to taste of turnips.

Pastry

200g plain flour

50g unrefined caster sugar

35g cocoa powder

125g butter, plus extra for greasing

2 egg yolks

Filling

500g mascarpone

3 tbsp runny honey

1 tsp vanilla extract

150ml double cream, very lightly whipped

For the top

350g strawberries, hulled and quartered

50g apricot jam, warmed gently and sieved to give a smooth glaze (add a few drops of hot water if necessary)

SERVES 8–10

To make the pastry, mix together all the dry ingredients. Rub in the butter with the tips of your fingers until the mixture resembles breadcrumbs. Then add the egg yolks and mix well. The pastry should come together into a ball at this point: if it looks very dry, add a little water. This pastry tends to be a little dry and hard to handle, but persevere – it's worth it! Place the pastry in a clean bowl, cover it with clingfilm and chill for 1 hour.

Preheat the oven to 180°C. Grease a 23cm round, 2.5cm deep loose-bottomed flan tin with butter. On a floured surface, roll the pastry to a thickness of about 5mm and use to line the prepared tin, allowing the pastry to hang over the sides a little. This pastry is quite soft, so you will need to patch up holes as necessary with leftovers. Prick the base a few times with a fork. Place a circle of greaseproof paper over the bottom of the case and fill it with dried beans. Bake blind for 25 minutes, then remove the beans and cook the case for a further 5 minutes. This helps to dry and crisp the pastry so that it has a satisfying snap when you cut through it with your fork.

To prepare the mascarpone filling, beat the mascarpone until soft. Stir in the honey and vanilla extract, then fold in the cream until well mixed.

When the case is completely cool, trim any excess pastry from around the edge of the tart. Fill with the mascarpone mixture, and top with the strawberries. Brush the apricot glaze over the top and serve.

Cheese

Irish Farmhouse cheeses are the best end to any dinner party – certainly the ones that I would like to get invited to. I love to see a really good cheese platter making its way to the centre of the table.

Indeed, The Yellow Door sent Tony and Bertie – who were in Armagh for another fraught meeting with the warring factions – a platter of perfectly ripe cheeses and other goodies while they were still around that boardroom table. Having had little to eat all day, at least all sides really enjoyed the artisan beauties.

I urge you to explore the pleasures of proper cheese: no unripe supermarket bargain choices, but those smelly, slightly discoloured examples in your local deli.

Buying Cheese

Buy properly matured cheeses close to their best before dates and fresh cheeses long before their best before dates. Keep them in their original wrapping in a sealed container in the fridge and store different types of cheese separately, so that strongly flavoured ones do not affect more delicate ones.

Buying cheese is not difficult; buying good cheese in peak condition is a little more tricky. To ensure long shelf life, supermarkets generally store fresh-from-the-mould cheeses. Even really good cheeses are sold far too young and have not developed much flavour or character.

Buy from an educated and reliable supplier, or do some homework and be prepared to mature the cheese from young. I could write a whole book on cheeses but other people – such as Patricia Michelson of La Fromagerie in *The Cheese Room* – have already done this very well.

Cheeses I Love

When presenting a platter of cheese, it is important to have different flavours, styles and textures alongside some essential accompaniments. I usually follow a format when matching the cheeses for a board:

1 hard cheese

1 soft cheese

1 goat's cheese

1 blue cheese

Depending on my guests' tastes and the time of the year, I find that working within this format is successful.

My favourite cheeses:

Cashel Blue (blue), Crozier Blue (blue), Bellingham Blue (blue), Wicklow Blue (blue), St Kilian (soft), Wicklow Baun (soft), Cooleeney (soft), Millens (softish), Glebe Brethan (hard), Hegarties Cheddar (hard), Durras (hard), Gabriel (hard), Desmond (hard), Gubbeen (hard), Corleggy (hard), Adrahan (semi-hard), St Tola (goat's), Ryefield (goat's), Mini Gabler (seasonal goat's).

You can find the names and addresses of all these cheese producers at www.irishcheese.ie.

How to Serve Them

My essential accompaniments include the following – but you should certainly add your own favourites. Choose something from each section:

Something sweet
quince jelly or paste
cranberry sauce
apple jelly
sweet onion relish or chutney
sweet figs or apricots

Something fresh and crunchy
apples or pears
radishes
celery sticks
chilled grapes

Something crusty
crusty bread
sourdough bread
walnut bread
French stick

Something wet
port, sherry or Madeira
sweet wines
red or white wines

Something crisp
Robert Dittie's biscuits
celery and black pepper biscuits
walnut oatcakes
Frank Hederman's smoked oatcakes
water biscuits
Fudges biscuits for cheese
Millar Damsel biscuits

When you are planning a feast or dinner party always remember to put the last first, that is take the cheese from the fridge, cover it with a clean tea towel, allow it to come to room temperature and breathe for at least 2 hours before serving. This allows the cheeses to get to the very best eating quality and flavour, and allows you to get on with the rest of the preparations.

I know that cheese is traditionally served with port, but all sorts of drinks go well with all sorts of cheese. The pairing of sweet wines – including port, sherry and Madeira – with fruit and cheeses can be marvellously moreish, stapling your guests to their chairs while they slowly and politely demolish both your cheese platter and the contents of your drinks cabinet.

I avoid serving sweet fruit with dry wine as the fruit makes the wine taste very tart by contrast. Pairing soft cheese with fresh and tangy white wine is marvellous, though, and definitely worth a try.

Cheese, Honey and Nuts

If you don't have time to create a full cheeseboard, but would like something easy and really tasty to finish the meal, why not try this classic European combination?

Choose your favourite hard cheese, such as Parmesan, Pecorino, Manchego or an Irish equivalent, like Desmond or Gabriel. Crumble it into chunks and serve it with really good runny honey and toasted pecans or walnuts.

Pour the honey into a saucer or flat dish. Dip chunks of cheese into the honey, top with a nut and eat. A little different, but incredibly good, this also works well with soft goat's cheese, although you'll need biscuits to hold the soft cheese before adding the honey and nuts.

Yellowman

Yellowman, or honeycomb, is a Northern Irish speciality and always on sale at the Ould Lammas Fair in Ballycastle. Kids of all ages love it dipped in chocolate and it makes a wonderful petits four to serve with coffee. You'll need a sugar thermometer for this recipe. It isn't difficult to make, but you must be extremely careful with the hot sugar mixture.

butter for greasing

350g caster sugar

2 tbsp Irish runny honey

85ml glucose

1 tbsp baking soda

MAKES ENOUGH FOR 20,
AS A PETITS FOUR

Line a 20 x 30cm Swiss roll tin with greaseproof paper, ensuring there is about 2cm paper standing above the rim of the tin, and grease the paper lightly with melted butter.

Place the sugar, honey and glucose in a large pan over a medium heat. Pour in 100ml of water and stir gently to dissolve the sugar. When the sugar has dissolved, stop stirring and allow the mixture to come steadily to the boil.

Using a sugar thermometer, boil the syrup until it reaches light caramel/hard crack stage, or 131°C. Quickly pour the mixture into a large metal bowl and whisk in the baking soda. Take great care as the mixture will triple in volume very quickly and will still be extremely hot.

Immediately pour the mixture into the lined tin and spread it out fairly evenly with a palette knife. Do not overwork. Allow to set, then cut into rough chunks and store in an airtight container.

Home-made Chocolate Truffles

People believe that home-made truffles are incredibly complicated to make, but this is a culinary myth. They are, in fact, quick and easy to prepare. Make this recipe and your dinner guests will be overwhelmed by your gastronomic genius, but probably so intimidated that they will never invite you back to theirs for dinner. (This is what happens to me.) Better still, make them and eat them all yourself just in case.

250g best quality plain chocolate (at least 60% cocoa solids)

50g clear runny honey

250ml double cream

good quality cocoa powder or chopped nuts for coating

SERVES 12 (OR 6 CHOCOHOLICS)

Chop the chocolate into small pieces and place it in a heatproof bowl with the honey.

Heat the double cream until it's just starting to boil, then pour it over the chocolate and honey. Stir to mix the chocolate into the cream. Allow to cool for around 30 minutes, until the mixture has set to a suitable consistency for piping.

Using a piping bag fitted with a 2cm nozzle, pipe the mixture onto a baking sheet in balls about the size of a large marble. Chill the truffles until set.

Roll the little chocolate orbs in cocoa powder or chopped nuts and present them in petit four cases.

Variations

You can flavour the truffles with about 2 tbsp brandy, whiskey, coffee or whatever you fancy. Remember to reduce the cream by the same volume of other flavouring you add to ensure that the mixture sets – put the flavouring in the measuring jug and make it up to 250ml with cream.

Parties

Baked Ham and Cashel Blue Irish Rarebit / Thai Red Curry Dressing / Sweet Chilli Tomato Jam / Sesame-seared Irish Scallops with Thai Dressing / Crab Cones with Creamed Corn and Coriander / Irish Breakfast Canapé / Thai Chicken Wontons / Black Pudding Wontons / Coconut Chilli Tiger Prawns / Baked Baby Potatoes with Mascarpone, Pancetta and Chives / Chicory with Roquefort, Walnuts and Sun-dried Cherries / Spiced Irish Lamb Skewers with Raita / Sloe Gin / Sloe Martini / Bitter Sloe Gin / Yellow Door Mulled Wine / Champagne Mojito / Champagne with Passionfruit and Thyme Syrup / Champagne Ginger Fizz

Useful Information for Parties

We've been involved with more parties than I can count over the years. Here are some useful hints and tips we've learned.

Wine

You can expect to get 4–5 glasses out of a bottle of wine, and 8–10 glasses from a bottle of champagne. When we're catering for a drinks reception lasting 2 hours, we usually allow ½ bottle of champagne or cava and 5–7 canapés per person. When arranging dinner parties, it's a good idea to allow 1 bottle of wine per person. We find that in autumn and winter, around 60 per cent of people will drink red wine, but that in spring and summer – if the weather is good – 60 per cent will want white. We also find that people drink a surprising amount of bottled water – at least 500–600ml per guest – with about one third choosing sparkling.

Canapés

There are a few key issues to consider when deciding whether or not to serve canapés:

Do I have enough time to serve them? Guests should be eagerly awaiting dinner, so canapés are served only to take the edge off their appetites and should be finished 45 minutes before dinner is served.

It's important to provide variety. A mixture of meat, fish and vegetarian canapés of different textures and colours is best and most attractive.

Do I have enough time and oven space for hot canapés? Hot canapés are very welcoming, especially on a winter's night, but serving them can mean that you spend most of your time in the kitchen. I suggest providing a mixture of hot and cold canapés so that you have time to welcome and chat to guests as well as cook.

Buffet Service

When catering for a party of twenty or more, a buffet can be the most efficient style of service. It offers your guests a good choice of food and allows them to decide how much to eat. It's important to avoid too much choice, though, as a large number of salads and hot dishes will look messy on guests' plates, and confuse the palate with lots of different flavours mixing together.

I find the following format is best: 1 red meat dish; 1 white meat dish; 1 fish or vegetarian dish; a starch, such as potatoes, rice or couscous; green salad; vegetable salad, such as tomato and feta; selection of breads, especially if you are serving stew, hotpot or casserole with lots of sauce.

Plated Meals

A well-presented plated meal is great for an intimate dinner party of no more than ten guests. Any more than that can be problematic in terms of getting everything cooked at the right time, especially considering the amount of space in a domestic oven. My advice is to plate the main part of your meal with its sauce, and perhaps a small accompaniment, and serve everything else in bowls for your guests to help themselves. This family service method will ensure that your food gets to the table hot, and allows your guests to get to interact with each other as they pass the extras around.

Baked Ham and Cashel Blue Irish Rarebit

This is my alternative to a classic Welsh rarebit. It works well as a snack or light lunch, served with some crisp salad leaves and a simple dressing, or as a simple canapé. You can prepare the rarebit in advance and then heat it up quickly in a hot oven when you're ready to serve it.

750ml milk

3 bay leaves and 6–8 parsley stalks, tied with string

½ onion, studded with cloves

75g butter, plus extra for cooking

75g plain flour

300g Cashel Blue cheese, crumbled

3 egg yolks

1 tbsp wholegrain mustard

salt and freshly ground white pepper

20 thin slices white bread, lightly toasted

10 slices baked ham

olive oil

MAKES 45 CANAPÉS

Pour the milk into a saucepan and add the bunch of bay and parsley, and the onion. Bring to the boil, then reduce the heat so that the milk simmers gently. Simmer over low heat while you make the roux.

Melt the 75g butter in a thick-bottomed pan. Add the flour and cook over medium heat, stirring all the time, for 2–3 minutes. Add the hot milk, a ladleful at a time, stirring well to incorporate each addition. Add the herbs and onion to the sauce once all the milk has been incorporated and simmer over a very low heat for about 30 minutes, stirring occasionally. Remove the herbs and onion.

Allow to cool for 10 minutes before mixing in the cheese, egg yolks and mustard. Season to taste, taking care with salt as the cheese is naturally salty.

Spread some cheese sauce on each slice of toast, to a thickness of about 5mm. Place a slice of ham on top of half the toasts, and sandwich with the remaining toasts, sauce-side down.

Heat the olive oil with a knob of butter in a frying pan over medium heat. Add the toasts and fry until golden brown on both sides, turning once. Cut into 9 equal small squares. Place two squares on each skewer and serve immediately. Alternatively, allow to cool and blast the toasts very briefly in a hot oven when you're ready to serve them.

Thai Red Curry Dressing

This is a fresh, lively and spicy dressing that is delicious with fish, chicken, pork, beef or even noodles and rice. It's one of my favourite home fridge items.

3 garlic cloves

1 red chilli, roughly chopped

3cm piece fresh root ginger, peeled and chopped

1 lemongrass stalk, white part only, chopped

salt and freshly ground black pepper

1 tsp red curry paste

4 tsp dark soy sauce

1 tsp nam pla (Thai fish sauce)

grated zest and juice of ½ lime

bunch of coriander leaves, chopped

1 tsp honey

100ml groundnut oil

Place the garlic, chilli, ginger, lemongrass and salt and pepper in a food processor and blitz to a paste. Add the curry paste, soy sauce, fish sauce, lime zest and juice, coriander, honey and oil and blitz again until everything is just combined. Add a little more oil if necessary – the mixture should have a soupy consistency. Serve or store in a covered container in the fridge. It will keep for about 2 weeks.

Sweet Chilli Tomato Jam

Great with chicken, oily fish or even just with breadsticks.

olive oil for cooking

knob of butter

3 garlic cloves, finely chopped

3 red chillies, deseeded and finely chopped

½ tsp ground cinnamon

½ tsp ground coriander

1.5kg ripe vine tomatoes, peeled, deseeded and chopped

3 tbsp sugar

squeeze of lemon juice

salt and freshly ground black pepper

Heat a large sauté pan or saucepan over medium heat. Add a splash of olive oil and the butter and fry the garlic and chilli until softened. Add the cinnamon and coriander and cook for another minute.

Add the tomatoes and sugar and reduce the heat. Cook until the tomatoes have reduced and formed a slightly sticky jam. Be careful not to burn the tomatoes – this can happen easily – but a little caramelisation is fine. Add the lemon juice and seasoning to taste. Serve immediately, or store in a covered container in the fridge for up to 2 weeks.

Sesame-seared Irish Scallops with Thai Dressing

I like to serve these beautiful scallops in Chinese-style ceramic spoons.

10 fresh king scallops

salt and freshly ground black pepper

1 egg white

3 tbsp sesame seeds

juice of ½ lemon or lime

4 tbsp Thai Red Curry Dressing (page 161)

olive oil for frying

5–6 Thai basil leaves, very finely sliced

SERVES 20

Prepare the scallops by removing the roe and the little tough muscle on the side. Slice them in half and season on one side. Whisk the egg white lightly and pour it into a saucer. Pour the sesame seeds into another saucer. Dip the unseasoned side of each scallop in egg white and then sesame seeds.

Have the lemon or lime juice ready, together with a plate lined with kitchen paper. Place 20 spoons in a row and place ½ teaspoon of curry dressing in each.

Heat a sauté pan over high heat. Add a little olive oil. Fry the scallops quickly in batches, 5 at a time. Cook the scallops, sesame-side down first, then turn them over with a palate knife to cook for a few seconds on the seasoned side. In total, the cooking time should be just 30–45 seconds. Drizzle with the lemon or lime juice and remove from the heat.

Drain on kichen paper before placing a scallop, sesame side up, on each spoon. Finally, place a small pinch of Thai basil on top of each scallop and serve immediately.

Crab Cones with Creamed Corn and Coriander

These dainty little cones can be filled with pretty much anything and they look really good. You can buy wonton wrappers in Chinese supermarkets, usually in the freezer section. If you don't have cream horn moulds, bake the wrappers in miniature patty tins or serve the filling on savoury croustade cases, made from bread.

100g white crab meat

1 small shallot, grated

40g sweetcorn, very finely chopped or blitzed briefly in a food processor

squeeze of lime juice

small bunch coriander leaves, chopped

splash of nam pla (Thai fish sauce)

1 tbsp Mayonnaise (page 34)

salt and freshly ground black pepper

olive oil for greasing

20 wonton wrappers

1 egg, beaten

SERVES 20

Mix the crab with the shallot, sweetcorn, lime juice, coriander, nam pla and mayonnaise. Season to taste. Cover and chill until required.

Preheat the oven to 190°C.

Lightly grease cream horn moulds with olive oil. Carefully wrap the wonton wrappers around the moulds, overlapping them and brushing the join with beaten egg to form a seal. Place on a baking sheet and bake in batches, upturned on a baking sheet, for about 10 minutes, until golden brown and crisp. Remove the wonton cones from the moulds carefully and set aside on a wire rack.

Using a small teaspoon or piping bag fitted with a plain nozzle, fill each cone with crab filling. Serve immediately. It's important not to allow the cones to sit around, or they will become soggy.

Variations

Salmon Tartare, Lemon and Caperberries
Finely chop some raw salmon and mix with a little Mayonnaise (page 34), lemon juice and caperberries.

Irish Breakfast Canapé

This novel little canapé is great fun and always goes down a storm.

5 slices potato bread

1 black pudding, cut into 5mm slices

4 pancetta rashers, very thinly sliced

olive oil for cooking

brown sauce or ketchup

20 quail's eggs

MAKES 20

Preheat the grill on high. Use a round cutter to stamp out circles of the potato bread, slightly smaller than the black pudding. Cook the pancetta under the grill until crisp, then break each slice into four pieces.

Heat a frying pan. Add a splash of olive oil and fry the black pudding and potato bread until browned on both sides and the pudding is cooked through – this should take 2–3 minutes.

To assemble the canapé, put the black pudding on the bottom. Add the circles of potato bread and a small squirt of ketchup or brown sauce. Place a small piece of pancetta on each one. You can prepare the mini Irish to this point in advance. If you are not serving them immediately, put the little stacks on a baking tray and place in a low oven (140–150ºC) to keep warm.

Fry the quail's eggs in a little olive oil in a frying pan over low heat. The whites should be set but the yolks should remain soft. Fry as many at a time as you can manage. Trim the eggs using a cutter that is slightly larger than the yolks. Put the eggs on top of the black pudding, potato bread and pancetta, and serve immediately.

Thai Chicken Wontons

1 skinless boneless chicken breast, diced and chilled

1 tsp salt

1 egg white

125ml double cream, chilled

1 red chilli, deseeded and finely chopped

small bunch of coriander leaves, chopped

1 garlic clove, finely chopped

1 tsp finely chopped fresh root ginger

1 lemongrass stalk, white part only, very finely chopped

grated zest and juice of ½ lime

dash of light soy sauce

dash of nam pla (Thai fish sauce)

freshly ground white pepper

1 pack of wonton wrappers

1 egg, beaten

vegetable oil for deep-frying

1 lime, cut into wedges, to serve

MAKES 45–50

Place the chicken, salt and egg white in a food processor and blitz until smooth. With the machine running, add the cream in a steady stream, but try to avoid overmixing. Transfer the chicken to a mixing bowl. Add the chilli, coriander, garlic, ginger, lemongrass, lime zest and juice, soy sauce and nam pla. Season with white pepper. Mix well with a wooden spoon and chill for at least 2 hours.

Lay the wonton wrappers on a board and brush the edges with beaten egg. Place a teaspoon of the chicken mixture in the centre of each wrapper and then fold the wrappers over, corner to corner to form a triangle, making sure there's no air left in the wonton.

Heat the oil for deep frying to 190°C. Deep fry the wontons in batches for 30–45 seconds on each side (a total of 1–1½ minutes). Drain on kitchen paper and serve as quickly as possible, with wedges of lime.

Variation

Thai Prawn Wontons

Use the same weight of shelled, deveined raw tiger prawns instead of the chicken. Proceed with the rest of the recipe in the same way.

Black Pudding Wontons

groundnut oil for frying

1 small onion, finely chopped

2 garlic cloves, finely chopped

1 tsp grated fresh root ginger

1 red chilli, deseeded and finely chopped

1 tsp ground cumin

150g belly pork, minced

125g black pudding, chopped or crumbled

2 spring onions, finely chopped

bunch of coriander leaves, chopped

splash of dark soy sauce

splash of sesame oil

salt and freshly ground black pepper

1 pack of wonton wrappers

1 egg, beaten

vegetable oil for deep-frying

MAKES 45–50

Heat a frying pan over medium heat. Add a splash of groundnut oil and heat briefly. Then add the onion, garlic, ginger and chilli and sauté. When softened, but not coloured, add the cumin and cook for a further 1–2 minutes. Remove from the pan, place in a mixing bowl and allow to cool.

Add the minced pork, black pudding, spring onions, coriander, soy sauce, sesame oil and seasoning. Mix well, and then use to fill the wonton wrappers and deep-fry as for Thai Chicken Wontons (opposite).

Coconut Chilli Tiger Prawns

Flour mix

125g plain flour

40g curry powder

1½ tsp salt

Egg mix

4 eggs

75ml milk

Coconut mix

100g desiccated coconut

100g toasted fine breadcrumbs, sieved

¼ tsp cayenne pepper

1 tsp dried dill

½ tsp dried chilli flakes

corn or vegetable oil for deep-frying

20–25 raw tiger prawns, peeled and deveined

MAKES 20-25

Prepare the mixes. Stir the flour, curry powder and salt together and place in a bowl. Whisk the eggs and milk in another bowl. Combine the coconut, breadcrumbs, cayenne, dill and chilli flakes in a third bowl.

Toss the prawns in the flour mix, then in the egg mix and finally in the crumb mixture to coat them evenly. Heat the oil for deep-frying to 185°C. Fry the coated prawns for 2–3 minutes until golden brown and really crispy. Drain on kitchen paper and serve with coriander and lime Aïoli (page 34).

Note: To avoid having fingers that resemble a frog's I would encourage you to use my dry hand, wet hand method: use one hand for the wet (egg) mix and another for the dry. Do not place your wet hand into the flour or coconut mixes or vice versa. This will ensure you work efficiently and it also prevents you from ruining the mixes by having wet egg mixture in your dry mixes. When having to pané 200–300 Tiger prawns this becomes important, and means you can save the dry mixes and store them in a tight-fitting container for use another day.

Baked Baby Potatoes
with Mascarpone, Pancetta and Chives

1kg baby potatoes

3 rosemary sprigs, leaves finely chopped

100ml olive oil

salt and freshly ground black pepper

300g pancetta, finely sliced

400g mascarpone

grated zest of 1 lemon

bunch of chives, finely chopped

SERVES 20

Preheat the oven to 180°C.

Using a melon baller, scoop the flesh out of each potato. Place the potato shells into a large bowl and add the rosemary, 75ml of the olive oil and seasoning. Using your hands, toss the potatoes until they are coated with oil. Place the potatoes in a roasting tray and bake for 35–40 minutes or until cooked through.

In the meantime, fry the pancetta in the remaining olive oil until crisp. Drain on kitchen paper and allow to cool. Break into small pieces. Mix the mascarpone, lemon zest, chives and pancetta together in a bowl. Don't overwork the mix or the mascarpone will stiffen.

Remove the baked potatoes from the oven and spoon a little of the mascarpone mixture into each one. Serve immediately.

Chicory with Roquefort, Walnuts and Sun-dried Cherries

If you can't find sun-dried cherries, go for sun-dried cranberries instead. The bitterness of the chicory in this recipes goes perfectly with the piquant cheese and the sweetness of the dried fruit. A great vegetarian canapé.

3 heads of chicory

300g Roquefort cheese

150g shelled walnuts

150g sun-dried cherries

SERVES 20

Pull the chicory leaves away from the base. You should end up with lots of boat-shaped leaves to act as the carriers for the other ingredients.

Using your fingers, crumble the Roquefort into a mixing bowl. Add the walnuts and cherries, and mix gently. Spoon the mixture into the chicory leaves and serve.

Spiced Irish Lamb Skewers with Raita

These little lamb canapés taste like really good kebabs – not the the two o'clock in the morning ones that go all over your shirt.

Spiced lamb

500g minced lamb

small bunch of coriander leaves, chopped

1 tsp ground cumin

1 tsp ground coriander

1 tsp paprika

½ tsp chilli powder

2 shallots, grated

2 garlic cloves, finely chopped

1 egg

2 tbsp fresh white breadcrumbs

salt and freshly ground black pepper

Raita

200ml plain yoghurt

small bunch of mint, chopped

¼ cucumber, peeled, deseeded and grated

squeeze of lemon juice

SERVES 20

Preheat the oven to 200°C.

Place the lamb, coriander leaves, cumin, ground coriander, paprika, chilli powder, grated shallots, garlic, eggs, breadcrumbs and seasoning in a bowl and mix until thoroughly combined.

Roll the mixture into balls, slightly smaller than golf balls, and place in a roasting tin. Bake in the oven for 6–7 minutes.

Meanwhile, make the raita. Mix the yoghurt, mint, cucumber and lemon with seasoning to taste.

When the lamb balls are cooked, put them onto skewers or cocktail sticks. Serve immediately, with the raita.

Sloes

What is it about discovering your very own stand of sloe bushes that is so exciting? Suddenly, secrecy becomes the order of the day and the weeks drag by until the sloes are ready to pick. Will the birds get to them before you, or, worse, another Sunday rambler? The satisfaction of returning home with scratched arms and a full bag of silver-dusted purpley fruit can only be matched by the pleasure of sipping your very own sloe gin after supper with good friends in the depths of the following winter.

A lot of recipes say that you should only pick after the first frost, or that you have to prick the sloes or freeze them before starting. I don't bother with any of this and still end up with delicious sloe gin.

Friends have experimented by adding vanilla pods and even star anise to their sloe gin but I am a purist and have always stuck to the classic recipe. Another twist is to drain the gin off after a few months and bottle it. Then add sherry to the sloes and start all over again. Two recipes for the price of one.

Sloe Gin

Buy good quality gin for this recipe but don't use your finest bottle.

450g sloes, thoroughly washed
200g unrefined caster sugar
750ml gin

Place the sloes in a Kilner jar or wide-necked bottle. Pour in the sugar and top up the bottle with gin. Seal the bottle, and shake it to mix everything together. Store in a cool dark place. Shake every day until the sugar dissolves (this will take a week or so). Taste after a couple of weeks, and add extra sugar if you like a more syrupy liqueur.

Variations

Damson Gin
If you find a stand of wild damsons these days you are lucky indeed, but this can be made with damsons from the garden or shop-bought ones. Make it in exactly the same way as the sloe version.

Cranberry Vodka
Substitute vodka for the gin and ripe cranberries for the sloes. Add a cinnamon stick and the zest (with no pith) of an unwaxed orange to the bottle. In a few months you will have a beautiful, pale pink vodka.

Blackcurrant Vodka
Again, follow the instructions for sloe gin, but replace the sloes with blackcurrants and the gin with vodka. Don't shake the bottle too vigorously, as the currants are delicate and break up much more easily than resilient sloes.

Sloe Martini

3 measures sloe gin

1 measure dry martini

squeeze of lemon juice

dash of Angostura bitters

crushed ice

twist of lemon or lime to decorate

SERVES 2

Simply shake all the ingredients together in a cocktail shaker and strain into martini glasses. Decorate with a twist of lemon or lime.

Bitter Sloe Gin

2 measures of sloe gin

2 measures of Dubonnet

1 measure of Cointreau

crushed ice

tonic or soda water, to top up

2 strips of orange peel

SERVES 2

Simply shake the gin, Dubonnet and Cointreau together in a cocktail shaker and strain into tumblers over crushed ice. Top up with soda or tonic water, and decorate with orange peel.

Yellow Door Mulled Wine

Mulled wine is great for a family Christmas get together. I love to serve it with mini mince pies and petit-four-sized Christmas puddings. Cheesy I know, but it certainly puts everyone in the festive mood.

450g unrefined brown sugar

3 vanilla pods, split lengthways

10 cloves

3 star anise

1–2 cinnamon sticks

grated zest and juice of 2 unwaxed oranges

grated zest and juice of 2 unwaxed lemons

4 bottles medium- to full-bodied red wine, Rioja, for example

500ml cranberry juice

1 orange, sliced

1 lemon, sliced

SERVES 20

Place the brown sugar, vanilla pods, cloves, star anise, cinnamon sticks, orange zest and juice, and lemon zest and juice in a pan. Bring to the boil, stirring to dissolve the sugar and simmer over low heat for 30 minutes to extract the flavour from the aromatics.

Place the wine, cranberry juice and sliced orange and lemon into another pan, then strain in the syrup. Place over medium heat and bring to the boil. Taste to check the sweetness and add more sugar as necessary.

Serve the mulled wine straight from the pan, or pour into jugs.

Variation

Non-alcoholic Mulled Wine
Use the same recipe to make drivers and kids feel part of the party, too: simply use grape juice instead of the wine and reduce the sugar by half.

Champagne Mojito

I first tasted this at Le Bar in the Plaza Athénée in Paris and was instantly hooked. Many happy nights of experimentation followed back at home. Double or triple up the quantities of stock syrup and store in the fridge – you will need it as your guests will definitely be asking for refills.

100g caster sugar

100ml water

2 bunches of mint

juice of 3 limes

4 measures Havana Club golden rum

crushed ice

1 bottle champagne to top up

lime wedges to decorate

SERVES 4

To make the stock syrup, place the sugar, water and 1 bunch of mint in a saucepan. Heat over a low heat. Once the sugar has dissolved, take the saucepan off the heat, cool and strain.

Half-fill a cocktail shaker with ice and add most of the remaining fresh mint.

Add the lime juice and rum along with about 50ml of stock syrup. Shake vigorously to release the full flavour of the mint.

Divide the rum mixture between 4 highballs filled with crushed ice and more fresh mint, and top up with champagne. Garnish with lime wedges.

Champagne with Passionfruit and Thyme Syrup

This lightly fragrant cocktail has an unusual but delicious herby background note. The cardamom and thyme work brilliantly together, but you could experiment with other herbs and spices. Rosemary and black pepper is a great combination, giving a slight heat for a lovely winter cocktail.

100g caster sugar

100ml water

2 cardamom pods, lightly crushed

2 thyme sprigs

4 passionfruit

1 bottle champagne to top up

SERVES 8–10

Make the stock syrup by dissolving the sugar in the water in a saucepan over low heat. Once the sugar has dissolved, take the saucepan off the heat. Add the cardamom pods, the thyme and the pulp of the passionfruit to the warm syrup. Leave to infuse and cool for 1 hour.

Strain through a fine sieve, pushing the pulp through and leaving the black seeds and the cardamom pod behind.

Add 25ml of flavoured syrup to each flute and top up with champagne.

Champagne Ginger Fizz

Another holiday discovery. As with the other champagne-based cocktails, don't use the best vintage – just go for any dryish, sparkling wine. The ginger adds low-level heat, which makes this perfect for an autumn or winter cocktail party. If you are feeling extravagant, serve this cocktail in a tall elegant highball with mint (or even Thai basil leaves), ice and a stalk of lemongrass to stir.

For a full-on Thai theme, add a halved chilli when making the stock syrup. Make sure it isn't too hot, though, as too much heat will kill the delicate mint and lemongrass flavours.

100g caster sugar

100ml water

5cm piece fresh root ginger, peeled and finely sliced

1 lemongrass stalk, lightly crushed

1 bottle of champagne

bunch of mint

SERVES 8–10

Make the stock syrup by placing the sugar, water, ginger and lemongrass in a saucepan over low heat. Once the sugar has dissolved, take the saucepan off the heat. Set aside to cool and then strain.

Add about 25ml syrup to each flute and top up with fizz. Decorate with mint leaves and serve.

Direct-ory

Some Favourite Suppliers, Delis and Speciality Food Shops

Andrews Flour
Belfast Mills
Percy Street
Belfast BT13 2HW
Tel. 028 9032 2451
www.andrewsflour.com
Flour

Arcadia
378 Lisburn Road
Belfast BT9 6GL
Tel. 028 9038 1779
Deli and speciality foods

Asia Supermarket
189 Ormeau Road
Belfast BT7 1SQ
Tel. 028 9032 6396
Speciality foods

Avoca Belfast
41 Arthur Street
Belfast BT1 4GB
Tel. 028 9027 9950
www.avoca.ie
Deli, speciality foods, cheeses and bakery

Burren Smokehouse
Lisdoonvarna
Co. Clare
Tel. +353 65 707 4432
www.burrensmokehouse.ie
Deli, speciality and smoked foods

City Food and Garden Market
St George's Market
12–20 East Bridge Street
Belfast BT1 3NQ
Tel. 028 9032 0202
www.belfastcity.gov.uk/
stgeorgesmarket
Speciality food market

Clydesdale and Morrow
581 Lisburn Road
Belfast BT9 7GS
Tel. 028 9066 2790
Cheese

Corn Dolly
Unit 7
Greenbank Industrial Estate
Newry
Co. Down BT34 2QU
Tel. 028 3026 0525
www.corndollyfoods.com
Bread

Country Choice Deli
25 Kenyon Street
Nenagh
Co. Tipperary
Tel. +353 67 32596
www.countrychoice.ie
Deli and speciality foods

Country Preserves
6 Aughanlig Park
Moy
Dungannon
Co. Tyrone BT71 6TE
Tel. 028 3889 1418
Jam

Deane's Deli
44 Bedford Street
Belfast BT2 7FF
Tel. 028 9024 8800
www.michaeldeane.co.uk
Deli and speciality foods

Deli on the Green
30 Linen Green
Moygashel
Dungannon
Co. Tyrone BT71 7HB
Tel. 028 8775 1775
www.delionthegreen.com
Deli and speciality foods

Ditty's Bakery
44 Main Street
Castledawson
Co. Derry BT45 8AB
Tel. 028 7946 8243
www.dittysbakery.com
Bread

Donnybrook Fair
89 Morehampton Road
Donnybrook
Dublin 4
Tel. +353 1 66 83556
www.donnybrookfair.ie
Deli and speciality foods

En-Place Foods
Crumlin
Silverstream
Co. Monaghan
Tel. +353 47 77033
www.en-placefoods.com
Chutneys and sauces

English Market
Princes Street/Patrick
Street/Grand Parade
Cork
Co. Cork
www.corkenglishmarket.ie
Speciality food market

Fallon and Byrne
11–17 Exchequer Street
Dublin 2
Tel. +353 1 47 21010
www.fallonandbyrne.com
Deli and speciality foods

Fivemiletown Creamery
14 Ballylurgan Road
Fivemiletown
Co. Tyrone BT75 0RX
Tel. 028 8952 1209
www.fivemiletown.com
Cheese

Frank Hederman
Belvelly Smoke House
Cobh
Co. Cork
Tel. +353 21 481 1089
www.frankhederman.com
Speciality and smoked foods

James Nicholson Wine Merchant
7–9 Killyleagh Street
Crossgar
Co. Down BT30 9DQ
Tel. 028 4483 0091
www.jnwine.com
Wines

Janet's Country Fayre
Unit 13B
Bullford Business Campus
Kilcoole
Co. Wicklow
Tel. +353 120 18008
www.janetscountryfayre.com
Chutneys and sauces

LA Drinks
3 Silverwood Industrial Area
Silverwood Road
Lurgan BT66 6LN
Tel. 028 3832 6601
Wines

McCartneys
56–58 Main Street
Moira
Co. Down BT67 0LQ
Tel. 028 9261 1422
Butcher

**Middleton Farmers'
Market**
Hospital Road
Middleton
Co. Cork
Tel. +353 21 463 1096
Speciality food market

Moyallon Foods
76 Crowhill Road
Craigavon
Co. Armagh BT66 7AT
Tel. 028 3834 9100
www.moyallonfoods.com
Meat, poultry and game

Mullan's Organic Farm
84 Ringsend Road
Limavady
Co. Derry BT49 0QJ
Tel. 028 7776 4940
www.mullansorganicfarm.com
Poultry and eggs

Neal's Yard
17 Shorts Gardens
Covent Garden
London WC2H 9UP
Tel. 020 7240 5700
www.nealsyarddairy.co.uk
Cheese

O'Doherty's Fine Meats
1 Belmore Street
Enniskillen
Co. Fermanagh
Tel. 028 6632 2152
www.blackbacon.com
Butcher

Picnic
47 High Street
Killyleagh
Co. Down BT30 9QF
Tel. 028 4482 8525
Deli and speciality foods

R&R Wine Merchants
Unit 9
M12 Business Park
Charlestown Road
Portadown
County Armagh BT63 5PW
Tel. 028 3833 2306
Wines

Sawyers
Unit 7
Fountain Centre
College Street
Belfast BT1 6ES
Tel. 028 9032 2021
www.sawyersltd.com
Deli and speciality foods

Sayell Foods
71 Fanshaw Street
London N1 6LA
Tel. 020 7256 1080
www.sayellfoods.co.uk
*Olive oil and Spanish
products*

**Sheridan's
Cheesemongers**
11 South Anne Street
Dublin 2
Tel. +353 1 679 3143
www.sheridanscheese
mongers.com
Cheese

Spice Deli
7–9 Market Street
Bangor
Co. Down BT20 4SP
Tel. 028 9147 7666
Deli and speciality foods

Swantons Gourmet Foods
639 Lisburn Road
Belfast BT9 7GT
Tel. 028 9068 3388
www.swantons.com
Deli and speciality foods

The Yellow Door
74 Woodhouse Street
Portadown
Co. Armagh BT62 1JL
Tel. 028 3835 3528
www.yellowdoordeli.co.uk
*Deli, speciality foods and
bread*

The Yellow Door
427 Lisburn Road
Belfast BT9 7EY
Tel. 028 9038 1961
www.yellowdoordeli.co.uk
*Deli, speciality foods and
bread*

Walter Ewing
124 Shankill Road
Belfast BT13 2BD
Tel. 028 9032 5534
Fish

**Other useful websites for
food lovers**

Board Bia
www.bordbia.ie

Eurotoques International
www.euro-toques.org

Invest NI
www.investni.com

Irish Farmhouse
Cheesemakers Association
www.irishcheese.ie

Irish Organic Farmers and
Growers Association
www.iofga.org

Rare Breeds Survival Trust
www.rbst.org.uk

Slow Food Ireland
www.slowfoodireland.com

The Soil Association
www.soilassociation.org

Index (numbers in italics refer to photographs)

A

aïoli, 34

almond croissants, 9

apples

apple and cinnamon scones, 45

pan-seared foie gras with caramelised apples and roasted hazelnut dressing, 80–1

puff pastry apple pie, 124

apricots

pain perdu with roasted apricots, 132–3

Armagh strawberry mascarpone tart with chocolate pastry, 146, *147*

aubergine and tomato salad, 36, *37*

B

bacon, *see also* pancetta

bacon and Cooleeney 'sort of' croissants, 8

cooking the Irish breakfast, 5

French toast, bacon and maple syrup, 13

late night breakfast, 19

leek, potato and bacon soup, 64

Bailey's

chocolate and Bailey's bread and butter pudding, 136

baked baby potatoes with mascarpone, pancetta and chives, 170

baked breakfast mushrooms or 'while-getting-the-papers' breakfast, 2

baked ham and Cashel Blue Irish rarebit, 160

baker's breakfast, 6, *7*

bananas

banana scones, 45

fried banana and maple syrup on toast, 12

barbecued langoustines with lime, coriander and smoked chilli, 65

barbecued spare ribs, 113

basil

basil mash, 89

griddled pineapple with basil and raspberries, 128, *129*

beans

flageolet bean stew, 99

late night breakfast, 19

béarnaise sauce, 121

beef

roast beef, 106

steak, 120

beetroot

Jilly's goat's cheese, beetroot and toasted pine nut salad, 75

bitter sloe gin, 176

black pudding

black pudding mash, 89

black pudding wontons, 167

braised potatoes with black pudding, 101

cooking the full Irish breakfast, 5

Irish breakfast canapé, 165

blackcurrant vodka, 175

Bloody Mary, 18

blueberry scones, 45

braised fennel, 100

braised potatoes with black pudding, 101

bread, 24–29

cheese and onion ciabatta, 31

chocolate and Bailey's bread and butter pudding, 136

ciabatta, 30–1

focaccia, 27–8

French toast, bacon and maple syrup, 13

fried banana and maple syrup on toast, 12

goat's cheese and roasted red pepper focaccia, 28

olive ciabatta, 31

pain perdu with roasted apricots, 132–3

pan bagnat, 32

panzanella, 33

Parmesan ciabatta, 31

rosemary and red onion focaccia, 28

simple, crusty, staple-of-life bread, 25–6

sun-dried tomato ciabatta, 31

breakfasts, 1–19

butternut squash

roasted spiced butternut squash soup, 62, *63*

buying cheese, 149

C

cabbage

pan-seared slow-cooked pork belly with creamed Savoy cabbage and whiskey and honey glaze, 83

cakes

chocolate brownies, 46, *47*

coconut and passionfruit slices, 49

flourless chocolate cake, 140, *141*

pistachio and olive oil cake, 130

yellowman and mascarpone cheesecake with chocolate sauce, 138

canapés

baked baby potatoes with mascarpone, pancetta and chives, 170

baked ham and Cashel Blue Irish rarebit, 160

black pudding wontons, 167

chicory with Roquefort, walnuts and sun-dried cherries, 171

coconut chilli tiger prawns, 168, *169*

cones with salmon tartare, lemon and caperberries, 164

crab cones with creamed corn and coriander, 164

Irish breakfast canapé, 165

spiced Irish lamb skewers with raita, 172, *173*

Thai chicken wontons, 166

Thai prawn wontons, 166

carpaccio of venison with pickled walnuts, parsley cress and horseradish crème fraîche, 82

carrots

Vichy carrots, 100

Cashel Blue tart, 56, *57*

celeriac

celeriac remoulade, 35

creamed celeriac mash, 102

champ, 89

champagne

champagne and ginger fizz, 181

champagne mojito, 178, *179*

champagne with passionfruit and thyme syrup,180

cheese, 148, *153*

Armagh strawberry mascarpone tart with chocolate pastry, 146, *147*

bacon and Cooleeney 'sort of' croissants, 8

baked baby potatoes with mascarpone, pancetta and chives, 170

baked ham and Cashel Blue Irish rarebit, 160

buying cheese, 149

Cashel Blue tart, 56, *57*

cheese and onion ciabatta, 31

cheese, honey and nuts, 152

cheeses I love and how to serve them, 150–1

chicory with Roquefort, walnuts and sun-dried cherries, 171

goat's cheese and roasted red pepper focaccia, 28

Jilly's goat's cheese, beetroot and toasted pine nut salad, 75

Little Gem, pear and Bellingham Blue salad with
toasted walnuts, 74
mushroom and Parmesan puffs with truffle
oil, 40
Parmesan ciabatta, 31
potato and Causeway cheese pancakes, 10, *11*
rich tomato and Parmesan soup, 60
ricotta pancakes, 131
Sauternes-poached figs with rosewater
mascarpone, 134, *135*
yellowman and mascarpone cheesecake with
chocolate sauce, 138
cheesecakes
yellowman and mascarpone cheesecake with
chocolate sauce, 138
cherries
cherry scones, 45
chicory with Roquefort, walnuts and sun-dried
cherries, 171
chicken
chicken liver pâté, 78
chicory with Roquefort, walnuts and sun-dried
cherries, 171
leek, potato and chicken soup, 64
roast chicken, 104, *105*
smoked chicken fillet, 66–7
Thai chicken wontons, 166
chilli
barbecued langoustines with lime, coriander and
smoked chilli, 65
chilli hot chocolate, 48
coconut chilli tiger prawns, 168, *169*
sweet chilli houmous, 22
sweet chilli tomato jam, 161
chives
baked baby potatoes with mascarpone, pancetta
and chives, 170
Dublin Bay prawn and chive tart with prawn and
lemon mayonnaise, 54–5
chocolate
Armagh strawberry mascarpone tart with
chocolate pastry, 146, *147*
chilli hot chocolate, 48
chocolate and Bailey's bread and butter
pudding, 136
chocolate brownies, 46, *47*
flourless chocolate cake, 140, *141*
home-made chocolate truffles, 155
raspberry and white chocolate muffins, 16, *17*
raspberry and white chocolate scones, 45
yellowman and mascarpone cheesecake with
chocolate sauce, 138
chorizo
chorizo mash, 89
spiced potato and chorizo salad, 38
ciabatta, 30–1
coconut
coconut and passionfruit slices, 49
coconut chilli tiger prawns, 168, *169*
coconut ice cream, 127
cocktails
bitter sloe gin, 176
Bloody Mary, 18
champagne and ginger fizz, 181
champagne mojito, 178, *179*
champagne with passionfruit and thyme syrup,180

sloe martini, 176
Yellow Door mulled wine, 177
cones with salmon tartare, lemon and
caperberries, 164
confit of duck, 110, *111*
cooking the Irish breakfast, 5
coriander
barbecued langoustines with lime, coriander and
smoked chilli, 65
coriander mash, 89
crab cones with creamed corn and coriander, 164
pan-fried cod with morcilla, sauté potatoes,
roasted vine tomatoes and coriander pesto, 86
saffron couscous with roasted peppers, toasted
almonds and coriander, 39
couscous
saffron couscous with roasted peppers, toasted
almonds and coriander, 3
crab cones with creamed corn and coriander, 164
cranberries
cranberry vodka, 175
duck confit pie with cranberries, 41
creamed celeriac mash, 102
crème brûlée
raspberry crème brûlée, 142
croissants
almond croissants, 9
bacon and Cooleeney 'sort of' croissants, 8

D
damson gin, 15
deli favourites, 21–49
Dublin Bay prawn and chive tart with prawn and
lemon mayonnaise, 54–5
duck
confit of duck, 110, *111*
duck confit pie with cranberries, 41
pan-seared Barbary duck fillets with leafy
greens, pomegranates and pomegranate
molasses dressing, 112
Paul's game terrine, 76, *77*

E
eel
smoked eel and pancetta salad, 68, *69*
eggs
cooking the Irish breakfast, 5
Irish breakfast canapé, 165
late night breakfast, 19
smoked salmon and scrambled eggs, 3
end of the meal, 123–155

F
fennel
braised fennel, 100
mussels with lemon and fennel, 95
figs
Sauternes-poached figs with rosewater
mascarpone, 134, *135*
first courses, 51–83
fish
cones with salmon tartare, lemon and
caperberries, 164
gravad lax of salmon, 70
Irish whiskey-marinated smoked salmon, 72
Italian fish pie, 92–3

leek, potato and smoked haddock soup, 64
pan-fried cod with morcilla, sauté potatoes,
roasted vine tomatoes and coriander pesto, 86
pan-fried sea bass with Puy lentils, 94
seafood stew with saffron and tomatoes, 87
seared salmon with saffron mash and warm leek
vinaigrette, 90, *91*
smoked eel and pancetta salad, 68, *69*
smoked salmon and scrambled eggs, 3
soused Lough Neagh pollen, 73
Thai fish cakes, 42, *43*
flageolet bean stew, 99
flourless chocolate cake, 140, *141*
focaccia, 27–8
foie gras
pan-seared foie gras with caramelised apples
and roasted hazelnut dressing, 80
French toast, bacon and maple syrup, 13
fried baby squid with garlic and lemon, 53
fried banana and maple syrup on toast, 12
full Irish breakfast, 4

G
game
carpaccio of venison with pickled walnuts,
parsley cress and horseradish crème fraîche, 82
confit of duck, 110, *111*
pan-seared Barbary duck fillets with leafy
greens, pomegranates and pomegranate
molasses dressing, 112
pan-seared woodpigeon with Puy lentils, lamb's
lettuce and roasted walnut dressing, 79
Paul's game terrine, 76, *77*
gin
bitter sloe gin, 175
damson gin, 175
sloe gin, 175
goat's cheese and roasted red pepper focaccia, 28
gravad lax of salmon, 70
griddled pineapple with basil and raspberries,
128, *129*

H
ham
baked ham and Cashel Blue Irish rarebit, 160
honey
cheese, honey and nuts, 152
home-made chocolate truffles, 155
pan-seared slow-cooked pork belly with creamed
Savoy cabbage and whiskey and honey glaze, 83
horseradish
carpaccio of venison with pickled walnuts,
parsley cress and horseradish crème fraîche, 82
horseradish panna cotta, 71
houmous, 22
sweet chilli houmous, 22
Thai green curry houmous, 22

I
ice cream
coconut ice cream, 127
maple syrup and nutmeg ice cream, 125
vanilla ice cream, 126
Irish breakfast canapé, 165
Irish whiskey-marinated smoked salmon, 72
Italian fish pie, 92–3

J

jam
rose petal jam, 15
strawberry jam, 14
sweet chilli tomato jam, 161
Jilly's goat's cheese, beetroot and toasted pine
nut salad, 75

L

lamb
lamb shanks with prunes, 116, *117*
roast lamb, 108–9
Shepherd's pie with root vegetable mash,
118–19
spiced Irish lamb skewers with raita, 172, *173*
late night breakfast, 19
leek
leek, potato and bacon soup, 64
leek, potato and chicken soup, 64
leek, potato and smoked haddock soup, 64
seared salmon with saffron mash and warm leek
vinaigrette, 90, *91*
vichyssoise, 61
lemon
cones with salmon tartare, lemon and
caperberries, 164
Dublin Bay prawn and chive tart with prawn and
lemon mayonnaise, 54–5
fried baby squid with garlic and lemon, 53
mussels with lemon and fennel, 95
lentils
pan-fried sea bass with Puy lentils, 94
pan-seared woodpigeon with Puy lentils, lamb's
lettuce and roasted walnut dressing, 79
lime
barbecued langoustines with lime, coriander and
smoked chilli, 65
Little Gem, pear and Bellingham Blue salad with
toasted walnuts, 74

M

main courses, 85–121
maple syrup
French toast, bacon and maple syrup, 13
fried banana and maple syrup on toast, 12
maple syrup and nutmeg ice cream, 125
martinis
sloe martini, 176
mash
basil mash, 89
black pudding mash, 89
champ, 89
chorizo mash, 89
coriander mash, 89
mash talk, 88
roast garlic mash, 89
rocket mash, 89
rosemary mash, 89
saffron mash, 89
shepherd's pie with root vegetable mash, 118–19
mayonnaise, 34
mint
champagne mojito, 178, *179*
pea and mint risotto, 96, *97*

muffins
raspberry and white chocolate muffins, 16, *17*
mushroom
baked breakfast mushrooms or 'while-getting-
the-papers' breakfast, 2
mushroom and Parmesan puffs with truffle
oil, 40
mushroom soup with Porcini and herbs, 59
mussels with lemon and fennel, 95

N

non-alchoholic mulled wine, 177
nuts
almond croissants, 9
carpaccio of venison with pickled walnuts,
parsley cress and horseradish crème fraîche, 82
cheese, honey and nuts, 152
chicory with Roquefort, walnuts and sun-dried
cherries, 171
Jilly's goat's cheese, beetroot and toasted pine
nut salad, 75
Little Gem, pear and Bellingham Blue salad with
toasted walnuts, 74
pan-seared foie gras with caramelised apples and
roasted hazelnut dressing, 80–1
pan-seared woodpigeon with Puy lentils, lamb's
lettuce and roasted walnut dressing, 79
pistachio and olive oil cake, 130
saffron couscous with roasted peppers, toasted
almonds and coriander, 39

O

olive ciabatta, 31

P

pain perdu with roasted apricots, 132–3
pan bagnat, 32
pan-fried cod with morcilla, sauté potatoes, roasted
vine tomatoes and coriander pesto, 86
pan-fried sea bass with Puy lentils, 94
pan-seared Barbary duck fillets with leafy greens,
pomegranates and pomegranate molasses
dressing, 112
pan-seared foie gras with caramelised apples and
roasted hazelnut dressing, 80–1
pan-seared slow-cooked pork belly with creamed
Savoy cabbage and whiskey and honey glaze, 83
pan-seared woodpigeon with Puy lentils, lamb's
lettuce and roasted walnut dressing, 79
pancakes
potato and causeway cheese pancakes, 10, *11*
ricotta pancakes, 131
pancetta, *see also* bacon
baked baby potatoes with mascarpone, pancetta
and chives, 170
smoked eel and pancetta salad, 68, *69*
panzanella, 33
parsley
carpaccio of venison with pickled walnuts,
parsley cress and horseradish crème fraîche, 82
parties, 156–181
passionfruit
champagne with passionfruit and thyme syrup,180
coconut and passionfruit slices, 49
passionfruit vacherin, 143

pâté
chicken liver pâté, 78
Paul's game terrine, 76, *77*
pea and mint risotto, 96, *97*
pear
Little Gem, pear and Bellingham Blue salad, 74
peppers
goat's cheese and roasted red pepper
focaccia, 28
saffron couscous with roasted peppers, toasted
almonds and coriander, 39
pies
duck confit pie with cranberries, 41
Italian fish pie, 92–3
potato pie, 98
puff pastry apple pie, 124
shepherd's pie with root vegetable mash, 118–19
pineapple
griddled pineapple with basil and raspberries,
128, *129*
pistachio and olive oil cake, 130
plums
Victoria plum clafoutis tart, 137
pomegranates
pan-seared Barbary duck fillets with leafy
greens, pomegranates and pomegranate
molasses dressing, 112
pork
barbecued spare ribs, 113
pan-seared slow-cooked pork belly with creamed
Savoy cabbage and whiskey and honey
glaze, 83
roast pork, 107
roast pork belly with roasties, 114–15
potatoes
baked baby potatoes with mascarpone,
pancetta and chives, 170
basil mash, 89
black pudding mash, 89
braised potatoes with black pudding, 101
chorizo mash, 89
coriander mash, 89
leek, potato and bacon soup, 64
leek, potato and chicken soup, 64
leek, potato and smoked haddock soup, 64
pan-fried cod with morcilla, sauté potatoes,
roasted vine tomatoes and coriander pesto, 86
potato and Causeway cheese pancakes, 10, *11*
potato pie, 98
roast garlic mash, 89
roast pork belly with roasties, 114–15
rocket mash, 89
rosemary mash, 89
saffron mash, 89
spiced potato and chorizo salad, 38
vichyssoise, 61
prunes
lamb shanks with prunes, 116, *117*
puff pastry apple pie, 124

R

raita
spiced Irish lamb skewers with raita, 172, *173*
raspberries
griddled pineapple with basil and raspberries,
128, *129*

raspberry and white chocolate muffins, 16, *17*
raspberry and white chocolate scones, 45
raspberry crème brûlée, 142
rhubarb galette, 139
rich tomato and Parmesan soup, 60
ricotta pancakes, 131
risotto
    pea and mint risotto, 96, *97*
roast beef, 106
roast chicken, 104, *105*
roast garlic mash, 89
roast lamb, 108–9
roast pork, 107
roast pork belly with roasties, 114–15
roasted spiced butternut squash soup, 62, *63*
roasts, 103
rocket mash, 89
rose petal jam, 15
rosewater
    Sauternes-poached figs with rosewater
        mascarpone, 134, *135*
rosemary
    rosemary and red onion focaccia, 28
    rosemary mash, 89

S
saffron
    saffron couscous with roasted peppers, toasted
        almonds and coriander, 39
    saffron mash, 89
    seafood stew with saffron and tomatoes, 87
    seared salmon with saffron mash and warm leek
        vinaigrette, 90, *91*
salads
    aubergine and tomato salad, 36, *37*
    celeriac remoulade, 35
    Jilly's goat's cheese, beetroot and toasted pine
        nut salad, 75
    Little Gem, pear and Bellingham Blue salad with
        toasted walnuts, 74
    saffron couscous with roasted peppers, toasted
        almonds and coriander, 39
    smoked eel and pancetta salad, 68, *69*
    spiced potato and chorizo salad, 38
sauces
    aïoli, 34
    Béarnaise sauce, 121
    mayonnaise, 34
Sauternes-poached figs with rosewater mascarpone,
    134, *135*
scones, 44–5
    apple and cinnamon scones, 45
    banana scones, 45
    blueberry scones, 45
    cherry scones, 45
    raspberry and white chocolate scones, 45
    sultana scones, 45
seafood stew with saffron and tomatoes, 87
seared salmon with saffron mash and warm leek
    vinaigrette, 90, *91*
sesame-seared Irish scallops with Thai dressing,
    162, *163*
shallot tart tatin with red wine and balsamic
    vinegar, 52
shellfish
    barbecued langoustines with lime, coriander and
        smoked chilli, 65

coconut chilli tiger prawns, 168, *169*
crab cones with creamed corn and coriander, 164
Dublin Bay prawn and chive tart with prawn and
    lemon mayonnaise, 54–5
mussels with lemon and fennel, 95
seafood stew with saffron and tomatoes, 87
sesame-seared Irish scallops with Thai
    dressing,162, *163*
Thai prawn wontons, 166
Shepherd's pie with root vegetable mash, 118–19
simple, crusty, staple-of-life bread, 25–6
sloes, 174
    bitter sloe gin, 176
    sloe gin, 175
    sloe martini, 176
smoked chicken fillet, 66–7
smoked eel and pancetta salad, 68, *69*
smoked salmon and scrambled eggs, 3
soup, 58
    leek, potato and bacon soup, 64
    leek, potato and chicken soup, 64
    leek, potato and smoked haddock soup, 64
    mushroom soup with porcini and herbs, 59
    rich tomato and Parmesan soup, 60
    roasted spiced butternut squash soup, 62, *63*
    soused Lough Neagh pollen, 73
    spiced Irish lamb skewers with raita, 172, *173*
    spiced potato and chorizo salad, 38
    vichyssoise, 61
squid
    fried baby squid with garlic and lemon, 53
steak, 120
strawberries
    Armagh strawberry mascarpone tart with
        chocolate pastry, 146, *147*
    strawberry jam, 14
    strawberry sorbet, 145
sultana scones, 45
summer pudding, 144
sun-blushed tomato tapenade, 23
sun-dried tomato ciabatta, 31
sweet chilli houmous, 22
sweet chilli tomato jam, 161
sweetcorn
    crab cones with creamed corn and coriander, 164

T
tapenade, 23
tarts
    Armagh strawberry mascarpone tart with
        chocolate pastry, 146, *147*
    Cashel Blue tart, 56, *57*
    Dublin Bay prawn and chive tart with prawn and
        lemon mayonnaise, 54–5
    rhubarb galette, 139
    shallot tart tatin with red wine and balsamic
        vinegar, 52
    Victoria plum clafoutis tart, 137
terrines
    Paul's game terrine, 76, *77*
Thai chicken wontons, 166
Thai fish cakes, 42, *43*
Thai green curry houmous, 22
Thai prawn wontons, 166
Thai red curry dressing, 161

thyme
    champagne with passionfruit and thyme
        syrup, 180
tomatoes
    aubergine and tomato salad, 36, *37*
    Bloody Mary, 18
    pan-fried cod with morcilla, sauté potatoes,
        roasted vine tomatoes and coriander pesto, 86
    rich tomato and Parmesan soup, 60
    seafood stew with saffron and tomatoes, 87
    sun-blushed tomato tapenade, 23
truffles
    home-made chocolate truffles, 155

U
useful information for parties, 158–9

V
vanilla ice cream, 126
venison
    carpaccio of venison with pickled walnuts,
        parsley cress and horseradish crème fraîche, 82
Vichy carrots, 100
vichyssoise, 61
Victoria plum clafoutis tart, 137
vodka
    blackcurrant vodka, 175
    cranberry vodka, 175

W
whiskey
    Irish whiskey-marinated smoked salmon, 72
    pan-seared slow-cooked pork belly with creamed
        Savoy cabbage and whiskey and honey
        glaze, 83
wine
    non-alcoholic mulled wine, 177
    Sauternes-poached figs with rosewater
        mascarpone, 134, *135*
    shallot tart tatin with red wine and balsamic
        vinegar, 52
    Yellow Door mulled wine, 177
wontons
    black pudding wontons, 167
    Thai chicken wontons, 166
    Thai prawn wontons, 166
woodpigeon
    pan-seared woodpigeon with Puy lentils, lamb's
        lettuce and roasted walnut dressing, 79

Y
Yellow Door mulled wine, 177
yellowman
    yellowman, 154
    yellowman and mascarpone cheesecake with
        chocolate sauce, 138

People Who Inspire Me

Thoughout my career I have been fortunate to experience some very happy times but also there have been lows when I have felt like throwing in the towel. Luckily I have had the great privilege to encounter some extraordinary people who keep me going and inspire me; driving me forward to learn new skills; to improve and redefine what we do at The Yellow Door. I would like to acknowledge a few of these very special people here and thank them for the contribution they have made to my life:

My dear wife Jilly who not only puts up with me, but inspires and educates me. Jilly's Company, Moyallon Foods, is one of my main suppliers of meat, game, cheese and other speciality products. I can honestly say that the quality of her products is outstanding. Her love for good food is awe-inspiring and I consider myself a very lucky man indeed to have married her.

My grandmother, whom I would probably blame for getting me interested in food in the first place. I still have such vivid memories of watching her bake bread, buns and cakes with great skill and confidence, and waiting to see how the goodies came out of the oven. I also remember hanging around until her back was turned so that I could, like a little mouse, pinch something. Much to her annoyance, I still nibble, although I am a considerably bigger mouse nowadays.

My family. I am lucky to come from a large and loving home, where we were always taught to work hard and, more importantly, to put our heart and soul into whatever we were doing. My brothers, sisters, cousins and wider family circle play a big part in making The Yellow Door a continued success that we can all be proud of.

Wendy Sayell, a dear friend now departed, who was a true lady in every sense of the word. She had a remarkable knowledge of food, and absolute dedication to the provenance and quality of ingredients. If there is a heaven, Wendy will be there, and I hope she is in charge of the food. A beautiful person sadly missed.

and thanks to . . .

The staff. A devoted team of like-minded individuals who work extremely hard, sometimes under difficult conditions and great pressure. They produce great food and service with enthusiasm and relish. I am continually impressed with their energy, dedication and drive to do their very best.

Our customers. One of the joys of running The Yellow Door is meeting and dealing with amazing people. I owe them enormous gratitude.

Our suppliers. The quality of the food we produce is down solely to these individuals. I strongly believe that having the freshest and highest quality ingredients available is vital to the success of our business. Thank you, and the cheque is in the post.

Paul Bailie. Special thanks to Paul, my operations manager, for encouraging me to write this book, and also for providing me with some of his own well-tested recipes. He is a great ally and a big-time foodie.

Michael Donaghy. Executive chef and friend, he has been involved with The Yellow Door from the start and we have spent many a blisteringly busy service shoulder to shoulder on the pass. He consistently produces food of the highest standard.

Helen Wright. The most patient editor ever. Thank you for your encouragement and for keeping me focused (a hard job).

www.yellowdoordeli.co.uk

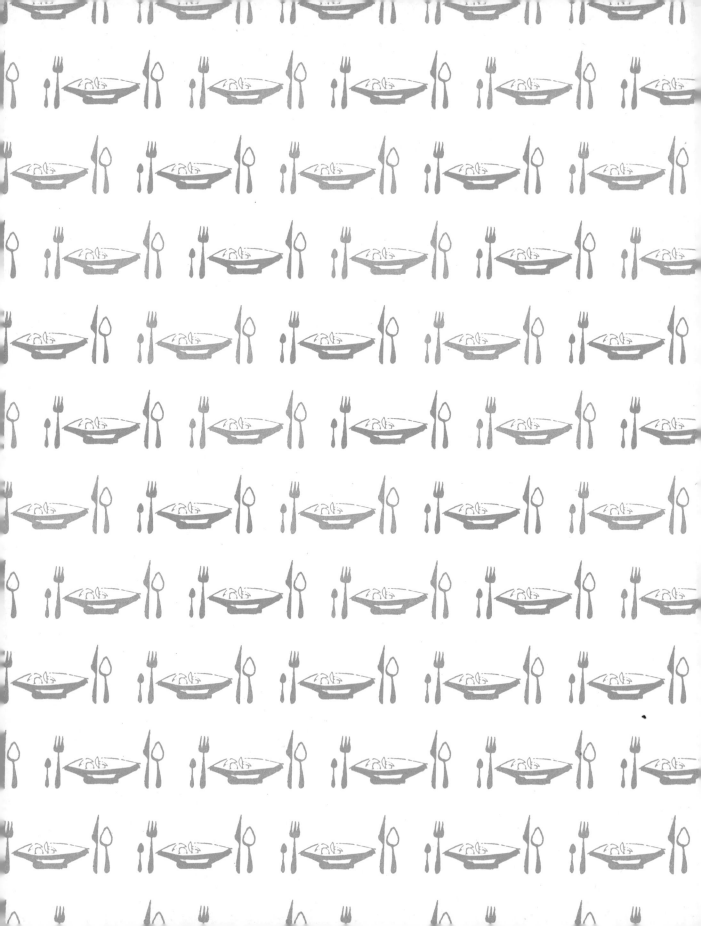